UNIVERSITÀ CARLO CATTANEO - LIUC

SCUOLA DI ECONOMIA E MANAGEMENT

Corso di Laurea in Made in Italy, management and entrepreneurship

OPENING A WINE PUB IN IRELAND:

a cultural challenge in the realm of beer

Relatore: Giuseppe Toscano

Tesi di Laurea di:
Mauro Tommaso De Candia
Matricola n° 18625

INDEX

1.Introduction

PART 1 - Introductory section

2. Internationalization of Italian wines

    2.1 World consumption

    2.2 Imports world market

    2.3 Italian exports

    2.4 Italian regions exports

    2.5 Production areas

3. Ireland

    3.1 An island in the ocean

    3.2 Natural parks

    3.3 Peat bogs

    3.4 Population

    3.5 Two jurisdictions

    3.6 Gaelic sports

    3.7 Economic growth and crisis

4. Cork city

    4.1 History

    4.2 North side

    4.3 City center

    4.4 South side

    4.5 West side

5. Mission

6. Entrepreneurial profiles

6.1 Mauro Tommaso De Candia profile

6.2 Maria Theresa Adams profile

6.3 Complementary profiles

PART 2 - Strategic section
7. Market analysis

7.1 Target customer

7.2 Customer's segmentation

7.3 Potential market size and growth prospects

8. Competitors

8.1 Direct competitors

8.2 Indirect competitors

8.3 Competitive advantage

9. Wine Pub

9.1 Layout

9.2 Tools

9.3 Furniture

9.4 Menu

9.5 Entertainment

PART 3 - Operative section
10. Marketing plan

10.1 Marketing materials

10.2 Promotions strategy

10.3 Online marketing strategy

11. Technical-production plan

11.1 Creation of the Wine Pub

11.2 Running the Wine Pub

12. Organizational plan

13. Economic-financial plan

14. Law and regulations

15. Conclusion

References

Appendix

1. INTRODUCTION

As is clear from the title, "Opening a Wine Pub in Ireland", this thesis is a business plan on a project which I am going to undertake in a few years. The idea of bringing the Italian wine in Ireland came to me accidentally one evening in April 2014 while I was having dinner in a Dublin's restaurant with an Italian girl and an Irish professor of philosophy who teaches in Lisbon, Portugal.

That night at dinner, the philosophy professor said to me and to the Italian girl that since he moved to Portugal he discovered his love for wine. In fact, he asked the waiter for the wine menu. Strangely, the "wine menu" had very little choice. I remember that there were only two red wines, a Sicilian Nero d'Avola and a French Bordeaux.

At this point, I decided to return to Ireland for a month in July 2014 for the sole purpose of "observing" the wine market. What I have noticed is that the wine in Ireland is very expensive due to excise duties and that most people are unaware of the various types of wine. During that month, I met Maria Theresa Adams in Cork, who became my current girlfriend. Thanks to her, I could learn more about the Irish way of life and their drinking habits. What I could understand is that wine is not within the Irish drinking habits mainly for cultural reasons.

The challenge that I would like to win is to convince the Irish people to drink Italian wine by serving it on tap in a Pub, a typical Irish place. This thesis is a business plan that will help me to win this challenge.

The thesis is divided in three parts: the introductory section, the strategic section and the operative section. The introductory section begins in chapter 2 with an analysis of statistical data on the internationalization of Italian wines. Afterwards, in chapter 3 there will be a description of Ireland. This chapter takes into account the geography, the population's culture, the legal system and the economy.

Chapter 4 is dedicated to the city of Cork, where I plan to open the Wine Pub. Chapter 5 describes the mission. Chapter 6 is about my partner Maria Theresa Adams and me. Here are described our entrepreneurial profiles with a reference to our work experience and how to combine our skills.
The strategic section starts in chapter 7 with a market analysis focused in knowing the best target customer. Chapter 8 identifies who are the main competitors. Chapter 9 is a detailed description of the Wine Pub.

Then, start the operative section in Chapter 10 which defines the marketing plan, which marketing tools to use and what promotion strategy to implement. Followed by a technical-production plan in Chapter 11 where it is explained in detail how to create the Wine Pub and how to run it. Chapter 12 is an organizational plan that defines who the key players are. Chapter 13 is an economic and financial plan based on estimates. Finally, Chapter 14 is a brief explanation of the Irish laws on corporate matters.

PART 1

Introductory section

2. INTERNATIONALIZATION OF ITALIAN WINES

The Italian wine industry, nowadays, has only one path to follow: internationalization and innovation. To do this, Nomisma[1], a company that deals with economic research, has created Wine Monitor[2], a tool to drive business abroad in the wine sector by providing information on market trends.

Wine consumption in the Italian market have been steadily falling, so internationalization is fundamental. In 2014, there was a record of wine sales abroad with a turnover of 5 billion Euros. According to Rolando Chiossi, Gruppo Italiano Vini[3], the only foreign market able to guarantee good margins of profits is the US, while Gianni Zonin, owner of Casa Vinicola Zonin[4], is interested in the Chinese market.

Not only internationalization matters, but also it is important innovation in the way of communicating. In fact, the CEO of Tenimenti Angelini[5], Emilio Pedron, is convinced that it is necessary to innovate the language of wine to intercept the new consumers.

It is also important to emphasize the designation of origin. In fact, according to Antonio Rallo, president of the Consorzio di Tutela Vini DOC Sicilia[6], international consumers reward the Doc label associated to the place of origin.[7]

2.1 WORLD CONSUMPTION

As can be seen in the table below, the top five countries for total consumption of wine in the world are the US, France, Italy, Germany and China. In the period 2013/2012, the total wine consumption grew by 24.0% in Romania, while it fell by 10.7% in Brazil. Over a period of ten years, between 2003 and 2013, the total consumption of wine grew by 41.1% in Sweden and 37.9% in China. In contrast, in the same decade there has been a sharp decline of -36.6% in Romania, -34.0% in Spain and -25.7% in Italy. As for the wine consumption per capita in 2013, on the first place, we find the French with 44.3 liters of wine per person, followed by the Portuguese with 43.4 liters of wine per person and in third place, there are the Italians with 36.5 liters of wine per person.

World wine consumption - 2013

| Countries | TOTAL CONSUMPTION | | | PC CONSUMPTION |
	2013	Var. 2013/12	Var. 2013/03	2013
	[.000 hl]	[%]	[%]	(liters)
United States	29.145	0,5%	22,5%	9,2
France	28.181	-6,9%	-17,3%	44,3
Italy	21.795	-3,7%	-25,7%	36,5
Germany	20.300	1,5%	2,9%	25,1
China	16.815	-3,8%	37,9%	1,2
United Kingdom	12.738	-0,5%	10,0%	19,9
Russia	10.933	-3,0%	25,9%	7,6
Argentina	10.337	2,8%	-16,2%	24,9
Spain	9.100	-2,2%	-34,0%	19,5
Australia	5.289	-2,0%	26,0%	22,7
Portugal	4.551	0,0%	-14,4%	43,4
South Africa	3.676	2,5%	6,2%	6,9
Netherlands	3.585	1,0%	0,6%	21,3
Brazil	3.488	-10,7%	13,4%	1,7
Romania	3.200	24,0%	-36,6%	15,0
Switzerland	2.650	0,6%	-10,7%	33,1
Sweden	2.120	0,0%	41,1%	22,0
World	238.700	0,6%	0,5%	3,4

Source: WineMonitor on OIV, Euromonitor International and IMF

Observing the trend of wine consumption in the last fifteen years in the map below, we can see that in Ireland, Czech Republic, Mexico and New Zealand there has been a growth in wine consumption by more than 150%. While there was a negative trend in countries like Italy, France, Spain, Portugal, Romania, Hungary, Argentina and South Africa.

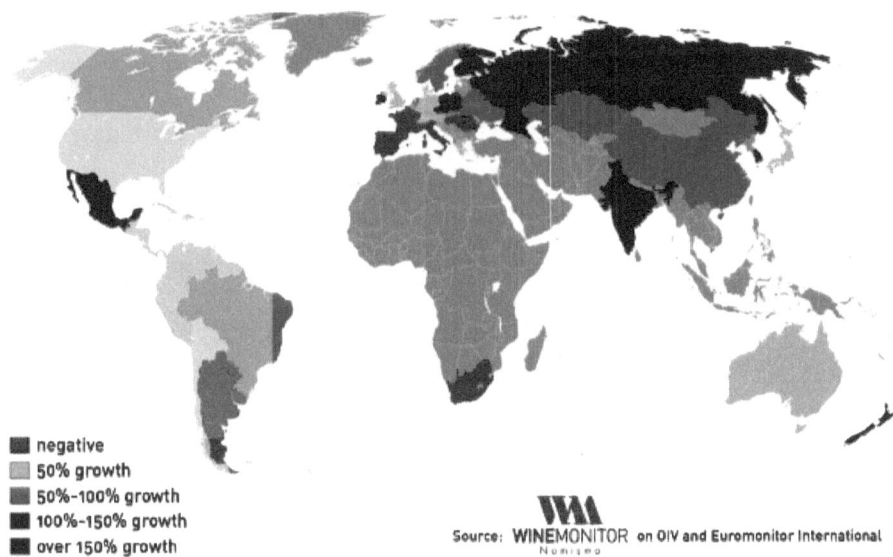

World wine consumption trend over the last 15 years (quantity)

- negative
- 50% growth
- 50%-100% growth
- 100%-150% growth
- over 150% growth

Source: WINEMONITOR on OIV and Euromonitor International

Knowing the target markets through market research, analysis of lifestyles, the use of social media, is a key factor in improving competitiveness. Often, however, Italian wine companies delegate to a distributor the export activities of their products without knowing their target market. Instead, it is important for wine producers get directly in touch with foreign consumers to be able to converse with them and influence them.

2.2 IMPORTS WORLD MARKET

N ow there is under discussion between the European Union and the United States the Transatlantic Trade and Investment Partnership (T-TIP)[8]. A treaty that aims to remove barriers to trade and investment in goods, services and agriculture between the European Union and the United States. The approval of this treaty will revitalize the Made in Italy and in particular, exports of Italian wine to the United States.

As can be seen in the table below, United States are the main importers of wine in the world. Imports of wine in the United States are growing, in fact, between the 2014/2013 grew by 2% and in ten years, from 2014/2004, imports increased by 47%. In the table will immediately notice the incredible growth of +2,611% in imports of wine in China in the decade 2014/2004, although between 2014/2013 has decreased by -2%.

World leading importers monitored: imported values (euro) and short and long term trends

Ranking		2014 wine imports (€ mln)	Var. 2014/2013	Var. 2014/2004
1	United States	4.032	2%	47%
2	UK	3.823	2%	13%
3	Germany	2.505	-3%	30%
4	Canada	1.465	-4%	100%
5	Japan	1.210	5%	44%
6	China	1.145	-2%	2611%
Other countries				
8	Switzerland	916	-3%	44%
10	Russia	865	-5%	177%
13	Sweden	602	2%	88%
19	Brazil	245	12%	244%

Source: WineMonitor

2.3 ITALIAN EXPORTS

A s mentioned before, the international wine market is changing radically. There is a decrease in consumption in the Italian territory, but as can be seen from the chart below, in the last ten years there has been a positive trend in the export of Italian wines. Exports increased from 1,392 tons in 2004 with a value of 2,840 million euro to 2,033 tons in 2014 with a value of 5,078 million euro.

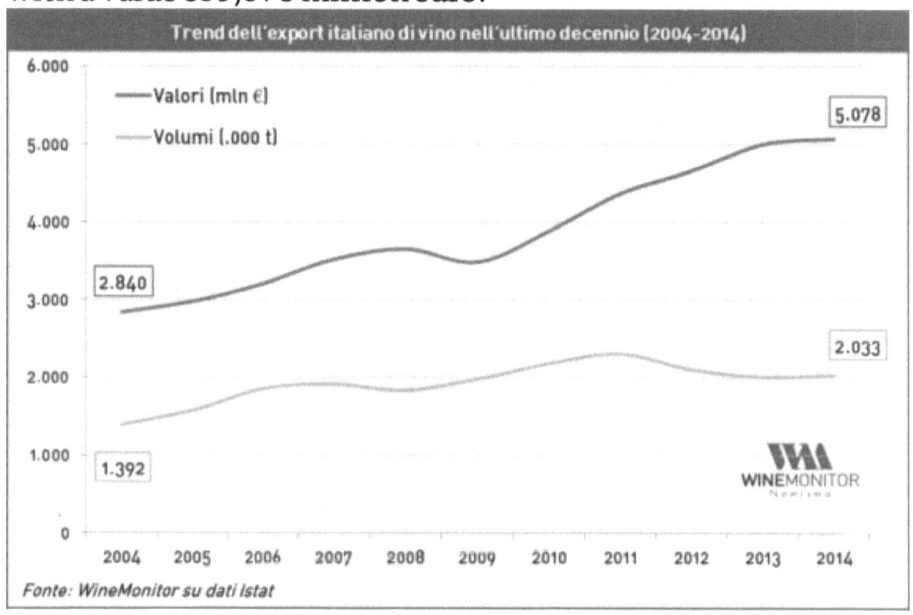

Trend dell'export italiano di vino nell'ultimo decennio (2004-2014)

— Valori (mln €)

— Volumi (.000 t)

5.078

2.840

2.033

1.392

WINEMONITOR

Fonte: WineMonitor su dati Istat

The main markets in which companies are exporting Italian wine are the United States (22%), Germany (19%), UK (13%), Switzerland (6%), Canada (5%), Japan (3%), Sweden (3%), Denmark (3%), France (3%), the Netherlands (2%), and Russia (2%).

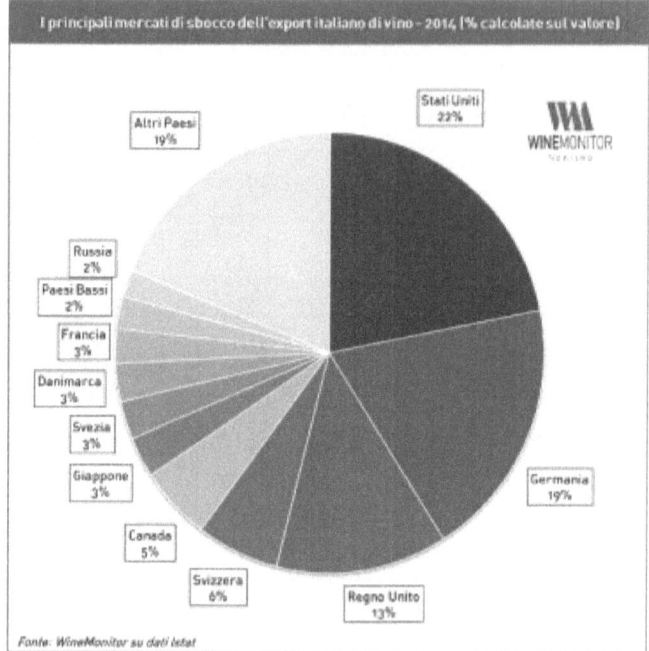

The most exported Italian wines are mainly bottled (76%), followed by sparkling wines (16%) and, finally, the bulk wines (8%).

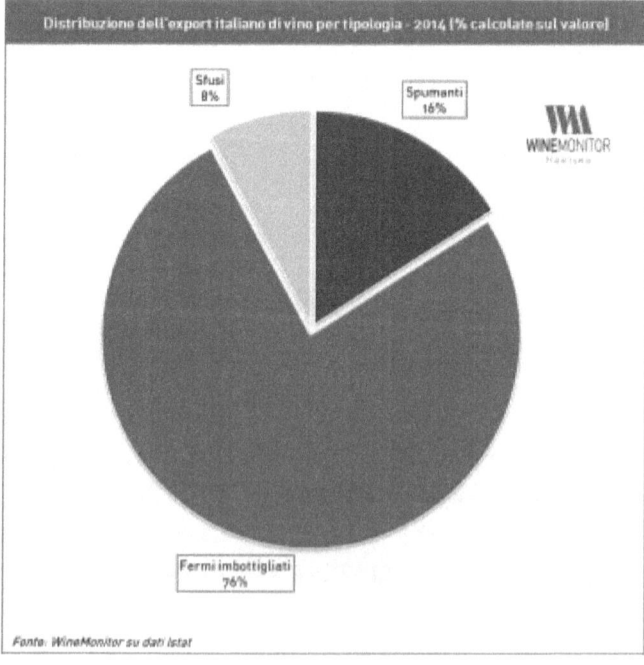

By analyzing the trend of export of Italian wines in the top five foreign markets between 2013 and 2014, it is to be noted that in the Anglo-Saxon countries like the United States and in the United Kingdom there was a slight increase in the quantity exported (+0.8% for the United States and + 0.5% for the UK). At the same time, a sharp increase in the value of wine exports (+4.4% for the US and +6.2% for the UK). This means that in these two countries are more and more appreciated wines of high quality. Instead, however, of what has happened in Germany and Canada where there was a slight increase in export volumes in Germany (+0,5%) while in Canada there has been a decline (-0.6%), but a sharp decline in the value of wine exports (-4.4% for Germany and -1.4% for Canada). These results suggest that in Germany and in Canada are consumed mainly poor quality wines. Excellent results in Switzerland where is growing the amount of Italian wine exported (+ 5.5%) and both the value (+ 2.0%).

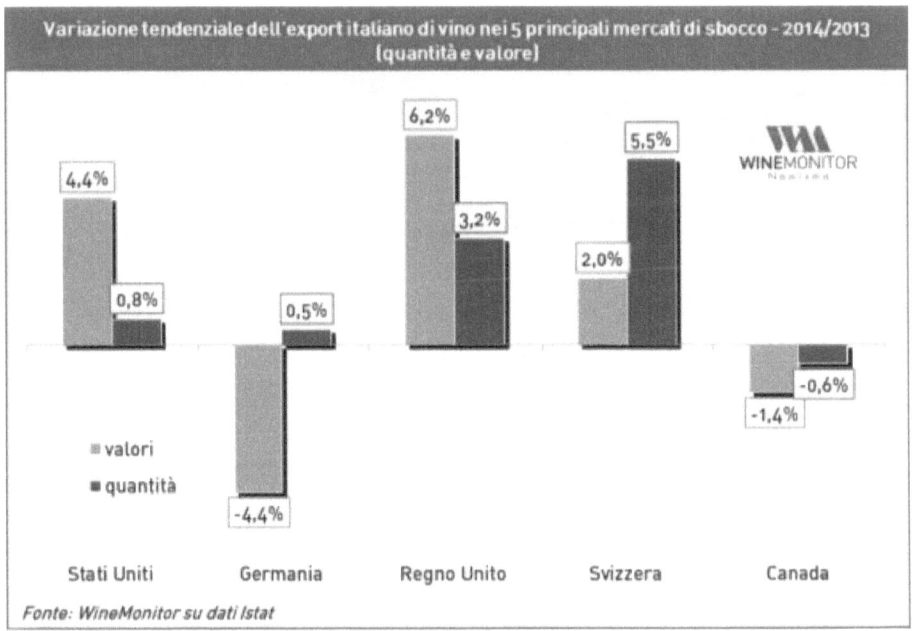

Looking at the variation of the type of Italian wines exported between 2013 and 2014 will immediately notice the incredible increase of sparkling wines in both quantity (+19.7%) and value

(+14.2%). Instead stable exports of bottled wines (-1.0% quantity and +1.3% value). Very negative result for bulk wine, which fell slightly in terms of quantity (-1.1%), but fell much in value (-17.3%). The two extremes, both positive and negative, balance the total export of Italian wines in a slight increase in both quantity (+1.1%) and value (+1.4%).

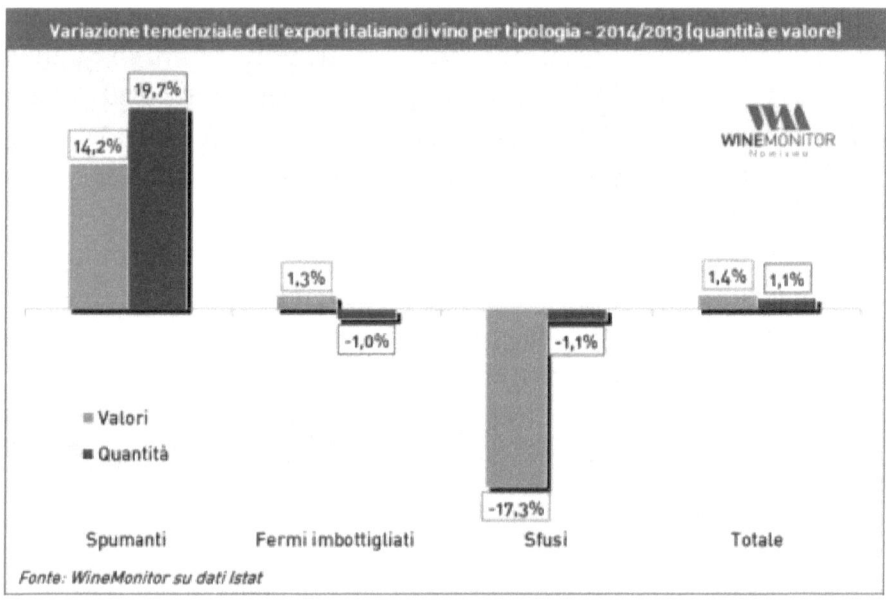

The main disadvantage of Italian wine export is to be fragmented into many small wine producers. This makes it difficult to have an adequate organizational structure and necessary skills for internationalization. The main obstacles to the export of Italian wines are managerial, such as lack of strategic skills, poor language skills, limited financial resources and lack of knowledge of foreign markets. Moreover, every foreign market is different from the other, so it is needed to make adequate segmentation according to different tastes, methods of consumption, distribution channels, laws and customs fees.

2.4 ITALIAN REGIONS EXPORTS

Associate the land of origin to wines exported makes foreign consumers become potential wine tourists to experience the Italian lifestyle, attracted by those places where their favorite wines are produced. Nowadays customers, anywhere in the world, are more and more demanding and to retain them is necessary that the customer has a 360-degree experience not only in consuming the product, but also in post-sale, being able to get in touch directly with the winery. A great tool is social media. If exploited correctly, social media allow customers to learn more about the winery and vice versa. This allows the establishment of long-term relationships between customers and the company.[9]

Le variazioni di breve e lungo periodo nell'export regionale di vino (valori)

Regioni	2014	VARIAZIONE 2014/2013	2014/2009
	(.000 €)	(%)	(%)
Veneto	1.669.654	5,2%	62,6%
Piemonte	984.821	1,6%	35,9%
Toscana	761.122	1,9%	49,4%
Trentino-Alto Adige	490.338	2,8%	25,7%
Emilia Romagna	309.396	-20,2%	38,9%
Lombardia	267.718	-0,9%	51,6%
Abruzzo	130.893	8,3%	46,4%
Sicilia	98.192	-0,6%	11,8%
Puglia	95.332	-0,2%	22,1%
Friuli-Venezia Giulia	91.445	20,2%	54,6%
Marche	51.125	0,7%	39,6%
Lazio	48.143	1,0%	48,4%
Campania	40.003	9,5%	77,0%
Umbria	28.486	5,4%	45,6%
Sardegna	23.602	1,0%	45,3%
Liguria	9.305	0,4%	28,4%
Calabria	4.710	-10,5%	24,0%
Molise	3.492	-28,3%	-29,7%
Basilicata	2.192	-7,2%	57,1%
Valle d'Aosta	1.419	-21,9%	143,4%
Totale Italia	5.112.085	1,4%	45,6%

Il dato Totale Italia è superiore alla somma dei valori regionali in quanto comprende anche i dati delle regioni i cui valori sono oscurati ai sensi della normativa sul segreto statistico.
Fonte: WineMonitor su dati Istat

In 2014, the Italian regions that export more wine are Veneto, Piedmont and Tuscany. Veneto and Piedmont together export more than half of all Italian wine exported. These two regions have had a positive trend in exports in the last two-year period 2014/2013, with a +5.2% in Veneto and +1.6% in Piedmont, and in five years between 2014/2009, with a +62.6% in Veneto and +35.9% in Piedmont. Wine exports down sharply in the 2014/2013, instead, for Molise (-28.3%), Val d'Aosta (-21.9%), Emilia Romagna (-20.2%), Calabria (-10.5%). Molise, in particular, has seen a sharp drop in wine exports over the long term, falling by -29.7% between 2014/2009.

2.5 PRODUCTION AREAS

Veneto is indeed the number one exporter of Italian wine abroad, but the first Italian wine-producing region is Puglia. In Puglia it is produced 19.9% of all Italian wines, while in Veneto is produced 18.7%. In addition, the amount of wine produced in Puglia has grown between 2013/2012 of +34.2%. Puglia, however, between the different regions of Italy, was ranked ninth in the export of wine. This means that most of the wine produced in Puglia is domestically consumed.

Produzione di vino in Italia per regione

	2011	2012	2013	var. 2013/12	Quota su prod. tot.
	(.000 hl)	(.000 hl)	(.000 hl)	%	%
Puglia	8.025	7.961	10.683	34,2%	19,9%
Veneto	9.481	9.257	10.068	8,8%	18,7%
Emilia Romagna	8.034	7.741	9.100	17,6%	16,9%
Sicilia	3.494	4.738	6.150	29,8%	11,4%
Abruzzo	2.733	3.203	2.946	-8,0%	5,5%
Piemonte	2.928	2.767	2.945	6,4%	5,5%
Toscana	2.569	2.172	2.447	12,7%	4,6%
Lombardia	1.678	1.388	1.594	14,9%	3,0%
Trentino Alto Adige	975	1.030	1.879	82,4%	3,5%
Friuli Venezia Giulia	1.290	1.283	1.459	13,7%	2,7%
Lazio	1.164	1.256	1.181	-5,9%	2,2%
Marche	880	871	1.018	16,8%	1,9%
Sardegna	522	505	602	19,3%	1,1%
Campania	690	662	753	13,7%	1,4%
Umbria	481	380	377	-0,7%	0,7%
Molise	175	182	260	43,3%	0,5%
Calabria	94	106	140	31,9%	0,3%
Basilicata	58	67	104	56,0%	0,2%
Liguria	41	35	35	0,5%	0,1%
Valle D'Aosta	16	14	18	31,2%	0,0%
Totale Italia	**45.325**	**45.618**	**53.759**	**17,8%**	**100%**

Fonte: WineMonitor su dati AGEA

In my dissertation, the target market is Ireland. Therefore, in the next chapter I will devote particular attention to this fascinating country.

3. IRELAND

I reland is an island in the Atlantic Ocean known as "Green Country" for its nature. The population is recovering well from a recent economic crisis preceded by a decade of economic boom. Around the cities is possible to see the effects of the housing boom in hotels and shopping centers. In the rest of the island dominates the wilderness. In Ireland, there is the highest concentration of people with red hair[10], it rains for most of the year and people drink tea at all hours. The northern region, the Ulster, still belongs to the United Kingdom, but among the population, there are no more violent conflicts.

3.1 AN ISLAND IN THE OCEAN

I reland is made up of a central lowland, Central Plain, surrounded by mountain ranges. The Central Plain was formed with sediments transported by the river Shannon, the longest river in Ireland. The plain is characterized by many small lakes, called "lough". The mountain ranges have modest heights, in the north stretches the chain Donegal, the Wicklow Mountains in the south and in the west the mountains of Kerry. The eastern coast, facing the UK, are flat, while the west coasts are quite jagged. The River Lee flows near the city of Cork and Shannon River flows near the city of Limerick. In the Atlantic coast, there is the archipelago of the Aran Islands, not far from the city of Galway. South of Galway there are the famous Cliffs of Moher.[11]

The Irish climate is very windy, rainy, and humid because of clouds from the Atlantic Ocean. Days are very variable. The maximum temperature rarely exceeds 20-Celsius degrees and the minimum temperature never drops below zero thanks to the warm currents from the Gulf.[12]

Figure 1 : Cliffs of Moher

3.2 NATURAL PARKS

Ireland is full of natural parks like Glenveagh National Park[13], nestled between the hills of Donegal and inhabited by deer, stoats and red grouse. In almost uninhabited area is located the Ballycroy National Park[14] which stretches for 11,000 hectares of lakes and grasslands. In the Southwest is located another natural oasis, the Connemara National Park[15], characterized by several peaks including the Twelve Bens. In County Clare is located the Burren National Park[16], characterized by a calcareous soil. In Killarney National Park[17], there are the Purple Mountains, so named for the color of heather flowering. In the Southeast of Ireland is located the Wicklow Mountains National Park[18], interesting for the presence of rare orchids.

3.3 PEAT BOGS

In Ireland, it is characteristic to smell the turf burning escaping from the chimneys, but a European Union directive prohibits the cutting of turf and using it as fuel. A fifth of Ireland is covered by peat bogs and the Irish people used peat for centuries. In fact, the European Union directive is not very respected by the Irish people.[19]

3.4 POPULATION

Because of a famine between 1846 and 1852, which caused the death of about two million people and the emigration to the United States of another two million people, the population of Ireland halved from 8 million to 4 million inhabitants[20]. The Irish population in the last twenty years has started to grow thanks to the arrest of the flow of migration to other countries and to a birth rate of 2.1 children per woman. It is estimated that in 2046, the number of inhabitants in Ireland returns like the one before the great famine.[21]

Catholicism has always been central to Ireland's national identity, affecting education, family and legislation. In Northern Ireland, the Catholic community is well separated from the Protestant one. In recent years, however, a number of child sexual abuse of Catholic priests[22] has ruined the reputation of the Catholic Church in Ireland, making it completely lose any kind of influence on Irish society, to the point that the population of Ireland has just voted in favor of a referendum for the legalization of gay marriage[23].

The official language of the Republic of Ireland is Gaelic and is taught in schools, but in reality, a minority of the population speaks it[24]. While English is spoken by the entire Irish population, even in literature. It can be seen the use of the Gaelic language in bilingual English-Gaelic road signs.

Thanks to a strong urbanization of Dublin and the surrounding areas[25], today in Ireland more than half of the population lives in cities. Among all the other Irish cities, Cork only exceeds one hundred thousand inhabitants. Small villages characterize the rest of Ireland.

Figure 2: Dublin city center

The capital, Dublin, is a city where buildings are restored, the harbor was modernized and the Phoenix Park is beautifully maintained. In Dublin, there is the brewery Guinness and the European headquarters of Microsoft. Many Italians travel to Dublin during summer to study the English language.

3.5 TWO JURISDICTIONS

Politically, Ireland is divided into two administrations: the Republic of Ireland and Northern Ireland (UK). The Republic of Ireland is a parliamentary republic since 1949 in which the President is elected for seven years by direct suffrage. Parliament, elected every five years, is made by the House of Representatives (166 members) and the Senate (60 members)[26]. The territory is divided into 4 provinces and 26 counties organized in twenty-six county councils, two city and county councils and three city councils[27]. The Northern Ireland is one of the four nations of the United Kingdom of Queen Elizabeth II. Northern Ireland Assembly is unicameral and has the power to legislate in many matters not pertaining to the Parliament of the United Kingdom[28].

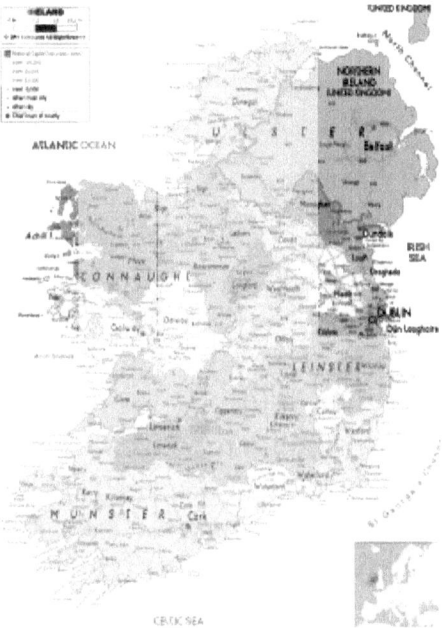

Figure 3 : Ireland political map. Source: http://
www.ezilon.com/maps/europe/ireland-maps.html

3.6 GAELIC SPORTS

The main sports organization in Ireland is the GAA, the Gaelic Athletic Association, founded in 1884 with the aim to promote the traditional sports like Gaelic Football, Hurling, Camogie, Handball and Rounders. Hurling is the Gaelic sport more popular and it seems to be one of the oldest sports in the world. Hurling is a team game and each team has 15 players. It uses a ball and sticks similar to those of Hockey.[29]

3.7 ECONOMIC GROWTH AND CRISIS

Following the entry, in 1973, in the European Economic Community, the country's economic situation began to change dramatically thanks to the funds allocated by the EEC. The impressive economic growth of Ireland made earn it the nickname "Celtic Tiger". The benefits of entry into the EEC were not only European funding, but also access to new export markets such as Germany, France and other member states. Within a few years, Ireland has gone from being one of the poorest countries in Europe to one of the richest, becoming from a country of emigrants to a country of immigrants from all over the world attracted by the economic boom.[30]

Another important element for the creation of the Celtic Tiger was the lowering of the tax burden. This has attracted in Ireland investments of US multinationals, like Microsoft and Google, who used Dublin as headquarters to enter the major European markets[31].

In the decade between 1992 and 2002, the GDP per capita has almost doubled, with a consequent increase in the consumption of goods and services. Currently the Irish GDP per capita has remained close to that of the richest countries of the OECD.[32]

In 2014, the Irish GDP was made up by 71.4% from services, employing 76% of the workforce, 27% from manufacturing, engaging 19% of the labor force and 1.6% from agriculture, engaging 5% of the workforce.[33] The tourism sector has been crucial to the Irish economic boom. The number of visitors per year varies from 6 to 8 million people from all over Europe and North America and annual revenue ranging from 3 to 5 million euro.[34]

Most Irish farms are almost all-small and medium size. According to the December 2014 CSO Livestock Survey[35], currently in Ireland there are 6.2 million cattle, 3.3 million sheep and 1.5 million pigs. The manufacturing sector in Ireland is composed of 30% by foreign companies from UK, United States, Germany, Japan, etc., that employ 45% of the workforce in the manufacturing sector and generate 60% of gross output.[36] Local products that are internationally successful are the Guinness and Jameson whiskey. Regarding the energy sector, Ireland is full of peat bogs and until recently, peat represented an important energy source for the country, but the European Union has banned the use. Consequently, Ireland has begun to take advantage of renewable energy such as wind, solar, tidal movement, and grass for the production of biogas.[37]

In 2004-2005, the growth of the Irish GDP was between 6% and 8%, falling to 5% in 2006, reaching zero in 2008, the beginning of the worst economic crisis in the Irish history. In 2008, the European Central Bank allocated funds to help Ireland, but in 2010 came the banking crisis. After that, the IMF lent 90 billion to the Irish Government on condition that the spending cuts take place. From 2011 onwards, the Irish GDP has started to grow again.[38]

Figure 4: Guinness factory in Dublin

In the next chapter, I will talk about the city in which I would like to start my own business: Cork.

4. CORK CITY

C ork, or Corcaigh in Gaelic, is the second city of the Republic of Ireland by population (123,000)[39]. The city developed on the banks of the River Lee around the medieval
monastery founded by St. Finbarr in the seventh century. The
River Lee has been of crucial importance for business in the city's
history. The city center is located in an island in the middle of
two river channels. The south bank of the river is flat, while the
north bank is hilly. The best of the city is lived at night in pubs
and restaurants. The best time to visit the city is in October and
November because there is the Jazz Festival[40] and the Cork Film
Festival[41].

Figure 5: Cork city. Source: http://www.corkcity.ie/aboutcork/

4.1 HISTORY

The Vikings, who founded their colony, attacked the monastery founded by St. Finbarr in the seventh century. In 1100, King MacCarthy conquered the Viking colony and Cork became part of the Kingdom of Desmond. In 1172, the Normans arrived in Cork from Wales and the king MacCarthy submitted to them. In 1500, the inhabitants of Cork rebelled to Queen Elizabeth I of England and the British repressed them. During the 1700s, the city had a strong economic development and grew in size. At that time, Cork became the main commercial center of the south coast of Ireland. During the Irish War of Independence (1919-1921), Cork was a major center of the conflict with the British. In the night between the 11th and 12th December 1920, the city was completely burned by the British.[42]

4.2 NORTH SIDE

On the north bank of the River Lee there is the Shandon neighborhood, dominated by the Anglican Church St. Anne's Shandon, built between 1722 and 1726. From the bell tower of the church can be seen all over the city. Opposite the church, there was the Butter Exchange, where between 1700 and 1800 it was decided the price of butter exported to Europe and America. Today, instead of Butter Exchange, there is the Cork Butter Museum[43].

4.3 CITY CENTER

In downtown Cork, the main street is St. Patrick's Street, dedicated to the patron saint of Ireland. On this street lined with shops and department stores, street artists often perform. In the building of the old Custom House, built in 1724 and operated until 1818, today there is the Crawford Art Gallery[44]. At the end of St. Patrick's Street, turn on Grand Parade, another main street of the center. On this road lies the historic English Market[45] in operation since 1788. Not far from the English Market, in Washington Street, the Court House is located in a building built in 1835. At the end of Grand Parade turns on South Mall, a street full of banks and offices. This road leads straight to the large building City Hall, which opened in 1936. A little further, there is the new Custom House in operation since 1818.

Figure 6: Cork city center, Oliver Plunkett Street

4.4 SOUTH SIDE

On the south bank of the River Lee, it can be observed the St. Finbarr's Cathedral, built between 1862 and 1876 by the British architect William Burges.

4.5 WEST SIDE

West of downtown, there is the largest park in Cork, Fitzgerald Park. North of the park, there is the old prison, Cork City Gaol[46]. To the south of the park, there is the UCC University College Cork[47].

5. MISSION

Given the increase of 150% of wine consumption in Ireland in the last fifteen years (paragraph 2.1 World consumption) and the need to find new innovative ways of internationalization of Italian wines, my business idea is to open a Wine Pub in Cork that combines the Italian tradition with the Irish one. The sale of wine would take place mainly through a system of tapping bulk wine to be consumed within the Wine Pub.

Figure 7: Drink System srl in Vinovo (TO), Italy, produces the system of tapping bulk wine **http://www.drinksystem.it/real.asp?IDCat=Vino**

My Irish partner, Maria Theresa Adams, resident in Cork and expert in the catering sector, will manage the activity of the Wine Pub operationally.

Our mission is to get used to the Irish people to consume Italian wines instead of beer, by creating a place familiar to the Irish Pub, where are served typical Italian products, particularly wine, with the entertainment of live music.

6. ENTREPRENEURIAL PROFILES

During one of many trips to Ireland, I met one day in July 2014, in Cork, the person who will become not only my life partner but also partner in the current business plan: Maria Theresa Adams. Our relationship has been kept alive over a year thanks to several trips back and forth between Milan and Cork. Before speaking about Maria, I would like to dedicate a few lines to talk about myself.

Figure 8: Mauro and Maria, Crosshaven, Cork, Ireland

6.1 MAURO TOMMASO DE CANDIA PROFILE

I was born in Cernusco sul Naviglio (MI), Italy, June 23, 1988. Due to several transfers of my family, I grew up in different regions of Italy, such as Lombardy, Emilia Romagna, Marche and Puglia.

I started working at 17 as an apprentice lithographer for a month, then with fixed-term contracts as receptionist, clerk of the store, warehouseman, call center operator, merchandiser and promoter. Meanwhile, I continued my studies in accountancy at an evening high school.

After finishing high school, I started working as second driver of my father's taxi. Meanwhile, I studied Business Administration at LIUC Carlo Cattaneo University[48].

In 2013, I obtained my bachelor's degree and I won through competition notice a taxi license. Since then, I am an independent taxi driver. In the meantime, I enrolled in the Master of Science "Made in Italy, Management and Entrepreneurship", and today I am writing this dissertation on a business plan that I intend to put in place at the end of my studies.

6.2 MARIA THERESA ADAMS PROFILE

Maria was born in Belfast, UK, October 20, 1975. At 14, Maria began working part-time as a waitress in few hotels in Belfast while studying at St. Monica high school. Later, she enrolled in a course in Childcare at Blackman Tech College[49] while she was teaching in a nursery school.

After college, Maria worked again as a waitress in several hotels in Belfast with fixed-term contracts until 2005, when she decided to move in Cork city, Republic of Ireland, because of the difficult political situation in Belfast.

Once in Cork, Maria worked as a waitress for four years at The Silver Key Bar and Restaurant[50]. Then, The Gresham Metropole Cork Hotel[51] hired her as a waitress where she worked for others four years. From 2013 until today, Maria works through temporary employment agencies as a waitress where temporary staff is required for events or peak workloads.

6.3 COMPLEMENTARY PROFILES

Our profiles complement each other regarding the business activity to be undertaken. Together, we can take care of the chores for which we are better prepared. Furthermore, the mutual trust at the basis of our relationship makes us aware that we can rely on each other, even in moments of difficulty.

My childhood and adolescence spent in various places opened my mind to the different mentality. My varied work experience made me develop a sense of intuition and adaptability to market changes. My studies in accountancy and my university studies formed me to run a business activity abroad on Italian products. My experience as a taxi driver has developed in me problem-solving skills in different situations in which I found myself. My role within the Wine Pub will be that of the general manager, director of business finances, accounting, marketing, relations with the public administration, banking relationships and relations with suppliers.

Maria's profile is very important because of her long experience as a waitress in the various hotels and restaurants. This makes her extremely competent in the field, with regard to not only the operational side and relations with customers, but also in the selection and training of the staff required to offer an efficient and high quality service in the Wine Pub. Moreover, since Maria is resident in Cork for over ten years and she is very friendly with everyone, she has as another value added a countless number of important contacts that she has developed over ten years of public relations on her job.

This combination of elements are the basis for the start of our business experience that has the purpose of bringing together the Italian culture with the Irish one.

PART 2

Strategic section

7. MARKET ANALYSIS

This section of my dissertation is intended to answer the question: "Who is my customer?" For any successful company it is important to understand what are the customer needs to be satisfied. Therefore, in the next few paragraphs I will define carefully: the target customer, customer's segmentation, needs to be satisfied, and the potential market size and growth prospects.

To know who is my target customer, what is his lifestyle, his buying preferences, what are his habits, what influences him in choosing and what are his wishes, I created a questionnaire to be filled by some people living in Cork.

Questionnaire for the Wine Pub's perfect customer

Age:........ Gender: [M] [F] Nationality:...................................

1) You are:

☐ Student

☐ Worker

☐ Retired

☐ Unemployed

2) Do you prefer:

☐ Red wine

☐ White wine

☐ Sparkling red wine

☐ Sparkling white wine

3) When you are in a Bar/Pub, do you buy:

☐ Glass of wine ☐ Bottle of wine

4) How many liters of wine you drink in a week?

☐ Between 0 to 1 ☐ Between 1 to 2 ☐ More than 2

5) At what time of the day do you drink wine?

☐ Morning: 5am – 12am ☐ Afternoon 12am – 6pm
☐ Evening 6pm – 11pm ☐ Night 11pm – 5am

6) Does the presence of a sommelier in the Bar/Pub influence your choice? (1 min, 10 max) ....

7) Does the presence of live music in the Bar/Pub influence your choice? (1 min, 10 max) ....

8) Does the presence of a TV screen in the Bar/Pub influence your choice? (1 min, 10 max) ....

9) Describe how it should be your ideal Bar/Pub

....

....

Figure 9: Questionnaire

7.1 TARGET CUSTOMER

Following my investigation of the market, which took place directly talking with the people I met in the city of Cork who filled the questionnaire, the target customer of my Wine Pub is an Irish man over 40 who lives and works in Cork city. Generally, people in Ireland had children very early during the beginning of the new millennium, on average about 30 years old[52], so they have now exceeded the age of 40, while their children are nowadays teenagers and do not require the presence of both parents at home to control them.

After the day's work, the target customer does not want to return home to his wife and to his troublemaker sons. Rather, he prefers to spend the evening in a friendly and quiet Wine Pub where he can relax peacefully, eat some finger foods accompanied by a glass of white wine and enjoy the live music.

In Cork, the whole working life, evening and nightlife, takes place mainly in the city center. Given that the target customer is working in the city center, he is already close to the Wine Pub where he will spend the evening. Most of the people in Cork primarily use public transport such as taxis and buses to return to their homes.

My target customer does not want to risk going in the wrong pub to spend the evening and eat bad food, drinking dirty water, then return home more stressed than before. For this reason, the staff within my Wine Pub will always be very friendly and helpful to customers, there will be fresh food every day and excellent wines.

7.2 CUSTOMER'S SEGMENTATION

Following my market analysis in Cork, I can divide potential customers by professional situation, gender and age. Regarding the professional situation, I have divided the potential customers in workers, unemployed, students and retired. After that, I have split for male and female. Later I have divided into age groups: minors, 18-24, 25-39, 40-59, over 60.

Workers

The target customer of the preceding paragraph falls under the category of male workers at an age between 40 and 59 years old. Customers belonging to this category prefer white wine, but they are also open to sparkling wines and red wines. When they are in a Wine Pub, they order primarily a single glass of wine, even though sometimes, they get a whole bottle. They usually come in the Wine Pub in the evening after work and someone stays up too late at night. These people really like the live music, and even to watch sports on a TV. They would listen willingly the advice of a sommelier.

A category similar to the previous one, but in reality very different, is that of male workers at an age between 25 and 39 years old. This category of people is a very narrow segment of the market because they have family commitments with their wives and young children. This prevents them to go assiduously to a Wine Pub. Nevertheless, these customers are one of the few categories that willingly consume red wine in more glasses. They too should be in the Wine Pub in the evening after work, but they do not want to have any kind of stress, they do not want the TV, they want to relax in peace with a quiet music in the background and claim that the staff is friendly and nice.

Remaining in the category of male workers, but down of age, between 18 and 24, we find, in addition to the Irish, the Scots who have a very similar culture. Both prefer a glass of white wine or sparkling wine, to drink in the evening after work in a relaxed atmosphere while enjoying the live music.

Moving on, however, to the category of female workers aged over 40 years old; there is a complete ignorance in the field of wine, but with the will to listen to the advice of a sommelier. This is a very narrow market, because Irish women, after work, do domestic services. For sure, these women, if they have time, they will go in the evening in the Wine Pub and they expect to find a clean place, eat good food and drink good wine.

Another tough market is that of female workers aged between 25 and 39 years old. Considering the fact that these women, in addition to working during the day and do domestic services, they must also take care of young children. This takes them all the time available during the day. If they had the opportunity to go to a Wine Pub, it would be at night, when their children have gone to sleep. The only wine they consume would be the sparkling wine. They really like the live music, and they expect to find a friendly environment not too noisy, but at the same time not too quiet, but mostly that, it stays open until late at night.

Going down of age, between 18 and 24 years old, in the category of female workers, there are girls in the early work experience, yet without family commitments that they would like to drink a few glasses of white wine in the evening after work. They would like to relax on a lounge chair in the garden, without spending too much and enjoy the live music in the midst of friendly people. The only problem in this category is the small number of people because most girls of that age are still university students.

Unemployed people

After talking extensively about the category of workers, I pass talking about the unemployed category. Currently, in Ireland, the unemployment rate is 9.9%, i.e. there are 212,000 unemployed[53]. Generally, people below 40 years old are more dynamic and can find work easily, so it is a frictional unemployment. The problem are those unemployed people who has overstepped 40 years old. For them to be able to find a new job becomes very complicated because age makes them less flexible and unattractive in the labor market. Therefore, I will focus my attention on unemployed customer segmentation over 40.

The retirement age[54] in Ireland is, on average, 65 years old. This age becomes the upper limit of the unemployed category, since exceeded that age they enter into the category of retired people. Within this category, there is a sub-category of unemployed, that is, those between 60 and 65 years. These people are completely out of the job market, even outside the black economy, and they are waiting to reach the retirement age. This category of customers is very narrow and has a very low purchasing power. These customers, even if they have a lot of time, they will never go in the Wine Pub for economic difficulties. However, they would like very low prices, a good atmosphere and a good selection of food.

As regards, however, the category of unemployed males between the ages of 40 and 59, they would consume many glasses of white wine throughout the day, as they have plenty of time. These customers generally because of their situation suffer from depression and this would make them feel happy in the Wine Pub to spend their savings from evening until the morning of the next day. They really like the live music, spending time with friends and eat something with good wine.

The category of unemployed females between 40 and 59 years old is a bit different from that of males, because they would go in the Wine Pub drinking a glass of white wine or a bottle of sparkling wine in the evening mainly as a distraction from the boring day as unemployed. They like the entertainment of live music and would like to find a friendly and good staff.

Students

It is time to talk about the category of students. This category is quite dangerous for several reasons. First, when it comes to students, we must refer to university students, because other students are considered still minors. In Ireland, it is prohibited to sell alcohol to minors[55]. So whenever you have to deal with students, you need to check the "National Age Card" to see if the student is an adult or not. This involves having someone at the entrance of the Wine Pub checking the documents of customers. Another element on the students to keep in mind is the fact that generally students are quite noisy, often they make fights with each other, break glasses and are disrespectful to objects that do not belong to them.

Students are new to alcohol; therefore, especially male students would order a whole bottle of red wine to show their manhood to female students who holding a glass of white wine or sparkling wine. They should be in the Wine Pub mainly during the evening and night. They like to listen to live music in a room with candles and high tables with stools.

During my investigation of the market, I wanted to let complete the questionnaire also to minors, since they will be the wine consumer of the future. If they could drink, they would choose mainly white wine, males would order a bottle while females only a glass. They should be in the Wine Pub in the evening and they would love to listen live music in a friendly and comfortable atmosphere, not too loud and not too bright.

Retired people

Finally, we came to talk about the category of retired people. As mentioned earlier, on average, in Ireland, people retire at 65, but it is not a fixed rule. There are also many retired people of 58 or 60 years old. It all depends on what is provided in the employment contract, where there are also provisions for retirement. However, this category is very different between males and females.

Among retired males is possible to find someone who still claims to be an Englishman, loyal to Queen Elizabeth II. Irish or British, the retired males are much attached to their beloved beer, but they willingly consume both red wine, white wine and sparkling wine. They should be in the Wine Pub in the afternoon and would remain there until late at night. Half of them are high consumers of alcohol. They would like the Wine Pub be welcoming and friendly, with a good staff, where they can talk quietly with their friends.

As for the retired females, they, like the retired males, consume various types of wine, red wine, white wine, sparkling wine, but in smaller quantities mainly by ordering a single glass. They should be in the Wine Pub in the evening and do not want any kind of nuisance. They will not hear a sommelier; they do not want live music and television. The only thing they want is to find a good team that knows good manners and would like that the Wine Pub is located within a hotel.

Those who receive a disability pension are a small niche in the category of retired people. These people could have any age. Because of their physical condition or mental hardship, they are high consumers of wine. They prefer the sparkling wine and they would go in the Wine Pub in the morning, because there are not too many people. They would like to listen to live music.

7.3 POTENTIAL MARKET SIZE AND GROWTH PROSPECTS

B eing a Wine Pub located in the city center, virtually all adult citizens of Cork may be customers, some of them regulars, others occasional. As shown in the graph below, approximately 70% of the Cork's population is an adult, so from 123,000 inhabitants, about 86,000 are potential customers. As regards, however, the "target customer", i.e. the male worker between 40 and 59 years old, always in the chart below can be deduced to be about 19% of the population, or approximately 23,000 people. Obviously, they are always "potential" numbers, therefore it may be that some of them do not drink, do not like the wine, do not go to the city center, and do not go in pubs. The actual figures are impossible to estimate, but certainly less than the potential.

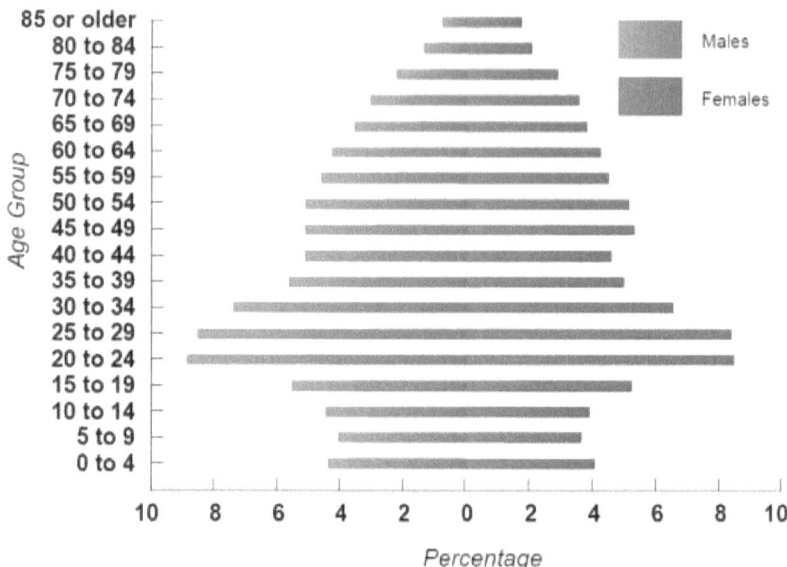

Figure 10: Source: Kelly, T., Hayes, P.; Cork City Profile 2014. Cork City Council, 2014; http://www.hse.ie/eng/services/news/Cork_City_Profile.pdf

One thing is certain; alcoholism in Cork is a serious problem because it affects many people. In particular, as can be seen from the graph below, the unemployed are those who drink more than others do. Certainly, the unemployed people will be the best customers of the Wine Pub, but they are not the "target customer". If this were so, a reduction in the unemployment rate would cause damage to the Wine Pub and vice versa.

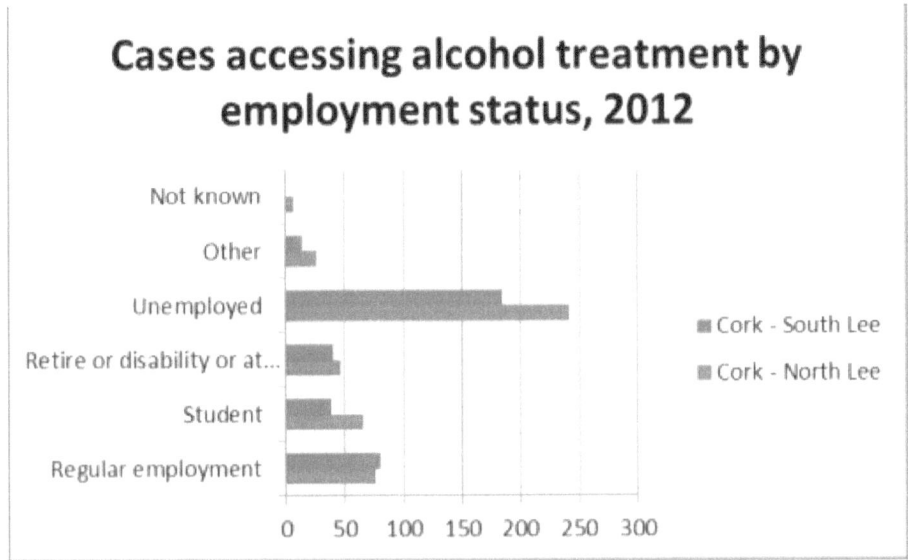

Figure 11: Source: Kelly, T., Hayes, P.; Cork City Profile 2014. Cork City Council, 2014; http://www.hse.ie/eng/services/news/Cork_City_Profile.pdf

Another element to consider is the impact of tourism on the Wine Pub. The Cork County Council has spent about 10 million euro in the last four years to promote tourism[56] and according to some surveys conducted by Fáilte Ireland, the Irish tourism office, hotels and restaurants expect an increase in turnover during 2015 and the following years[57].

8. COMPETITORS

In competition analysis to my Wine Pub, I prefer to classify competitors in direct and indirect. Direct competitors are those who offer a product/service very similar to mine, the indirect competitors are those that offer products/services diverse from mine but that attract towards them my potential customers. All competitors listed below are located in Cork city center.

8.1 DIRECT COMPETITORS

The Oliver Plunkett[58]: This Irish Pub is my muse. Personally, I spent many nights in this place to enjoy the entertainment of live music with a glass of beer. What I want to create with my Wine Pub is very similar to The Oliver Plunkett, with the only difference that will be served mainly Italian wine instead of beer. The main feature of The Oliver Plunkett is that there is live music of all kinds 7 nights a week. In addition, if a customer is hungry, there is also the opportunity to order food. At The Oliver Plunkett, you can order a glass of wine, but the variety is scarce. Upstairs there is a section dedicated to lovers of whiskey "The Frisky Irish Bar" always with live music entertainment. This inspires me to create a section within the Wine Pub dedicated to grappa. Another feature of The Oliver Plunkett is the opportunity to book party in the Pub through contacts provided within their website.

Figure 12: The Oliver Plunkett

Arthur Mayne[59]: This wine pub belongs to the chain "Cork Heritage Pubs". Before becoming a wine pub, Arthur Mayne was a pharmacy. The space inside is very limited and there are few places to sit. You can also order food throughout the day. The most innovative part consists in having adopted the Enomatic system, produced by the Italian company Enomatic srl, which consists in tap wine from the bottle to the glass through an automated system. Customers who want to buy a glass of wine with this system, they have to buy a prepaid card with € 20 credit from the bar and put it in the Enomatic machine. This Enomatic system is interesting and I am going to put it in my Wine Pub. Arthur Mayne is connected with a rear access to Crane Lane Theatre where there is live music 7 nights a week. The Crane Lane Theatre through this link provides the customers to Arthur Mayne.

*Figure 13: Enomatic system produced by Enomatic srl **http:// www.enomatic.it/new/default.asp?catIDPadre=33&catID=34&NewsLan=ENG***

Crane Lane Theatre[60]: It belongs to the chain "Cork Heritage Pubs" and it is physically connected with other three bars, the Arthur Mayne, The Stage Door and The Crystal Room. At Crane Lane Theatre, there is live music every night like Jazz, Blues and Burlesque.

Orso[61]: This is a café located right next to Arthur Mayne that in the evening it closes at 22:30. During the day, it serves food and has a small menu of wines. Along with the Arthur Mayne and the Crane Lane Theatre, they form a district where customers can eat and drink a glass of wine at the Orso, then enjoy the entertainment at the Crane Lane Theatre, and taste a variety of wines at the Arthur Mayne.

L'Atitude 51[62]: This wine café has a wide selection of wines and a few dishes to be associated with wine. Each week, on the upper floor, there are wine tasting events and live music.

The Woodford[63]: This bar is located in a building that was owned by a wine merchant Woodford Bourne & Co. Today, The Woodford Bar serves drinks and food. On Friday night and Saturday night, there is a DJ and the opportunity to dance. You can also book private parties with up to 50 people.

Meades 126[64]: This wine bar, situated in a good location and open only in the evening after 17, has an extensive menu of wine and a couple of dishes with salami and cheese.

Il Padrino[65]: Quite expensive Italian restaurant with an extensive wine selection. Inside this restaurant was recently opened a wine bar called "The Cellar".

Jacques Restaurant[66]: This restaurant in the heart of Cork, in thirty years, has consolidated business relationships with its local and international suppliers and it directly imports wines from small producers.

Bodega[67]: This is a nightclub on Friday nights and Saturday nights and a restaurant during the rest of the week. The Bodega is located in the building of the old St. Peter's Market. The term "Bodega" in Spanish means "winery", in fact you can order a wide range of wines.

El Vino[68]: This is a new wine bar & restaurant with two locations, one in downtown Cork and the other in the affluent neighborhood Douglas, who has Spanish cuisine.

8.2 INDIRECT COMPETITORS

An Brog[69]: This pub has existed since 1992 and has a DJ playing every night. In 2013, it was renovated but many people complain about the unfriendly behavior of the staff.

Reardens[70]: This bar is famous for live music and the opportunity to watch sports on television.

The Long Valley[71]: Historical Irish Pub greatly appreciated by customers.

Sin é[72]: This is another pub belonging to the chain "Cork Heritage Pubs". In this pub, every night there is live traditional Irish music.

The Bailey[73]: This bar survives mainly thanks to private functions organized inside.

The Oval[74]: Another pub belonging to the chain "Cork Heritage Pubs". The main feature of this pub is the interior design style of the early '900.

Franciscan Well Brewery[75]: This brewery is located in an old Franciscan monastery. The brewery serves beer brewed in it and the real Italian pizza.

Le Chateau Bar: This bar only exploits being positioned on St. Patrick Street, the main street of the city center. The owners are very criticized by customers for their rude behavior.

Mutton Lane Inn[76]: One of the oldest pubs in Cork belonging to the chain "Cork Heritage Pubs".

Sober Lane[77]: Pub run by young boys with a base in Cork and a new one in Dublin.

Electric[78]: This is a fish bar and restaurant well known in Cork.

Old Oak: Pub with a DJ playing every night.

8.3 COMPETITIVE ADVANTAGE

By investigating how the competitors are working, it is possible to learn to avoid their mistakes and imitate their strengths. As I mentioned before, The Oliver Plunkett is my muse regarding the style and the live music that there will be in my Wine Pub. Thanks to the Arthur Mayne, I discovered the existence of the Enomatic system. Given the limited space inside the Arthur Mayne, the Enomatic system was placed in a narrow corridor where it becomes difficult to notice it and even to use it. My strength will be to have a large space where to seat customers and the Enomatic system will be located in a central area easy to access to it.

The main thing is that no one in Cork, and perhaps no one in Ireland, has the system of tapping bulk wine mentioned in the "Mission" paragraph. This makes my Wine Pub unique compared to competitors. In addition, the association of some typical Italian dishes with good wine makes my Wine Pub competitive even for the best restaurants in town. Besides the quality of wine and food, the main difference between my Wine Pub and competitors will be given by the extreme friendliness and kindness of my staff who will be strictly selected and continuously monitored.

9. WINE PUB

Finally, it came the time to describe how it will be my Wine Pub. First, it will be located in the center of Cork. It will be precisely in the area between St. Patrick Street, South Mall, Grand Parade and Oliver Plunkett Street. In this area, there is always nightlife seven days a week.

My Wine Pub will be a place for those who want to relax while listening to live music. There will be high tables with wooden stools on the side near the bar and comfortable sofas with low tables on the opposite side. At each table, there will be a candle. The furniture will have a classic style.

At the bar, there will be a system of tapping bulk wine and, in the middle of the room, there will be the Enomatic system. A corner of the bar will be dedicated to grappa. The musicians who will perform each night will occupy a space at the end of the room where there will be a piano and all the necessary material for the various performances.

The Wine Pub will be open from 4 pm to 2 am to accommodate everyone who wants to find a place to relax after a busy working day. The brightness of the Wine Pub will be not too high and not too low, just enough to be easy on the eyes. There will be an extensive menu of wines and other beverages, fingers food and some typical Italian dishes. The prices of the wines and the food will be accessible to all income groups. The most important quality of my Wine Pub will be the kindness and friendliness of all the staff to customers. Guests will feel right at home.

9.1 LAYOUT

Below a picture of how it will be roughly the layout of my Wine Pub. The dimensions of furniture are not in the exact scale. Obviously, this is only a model to be adapted to the real space in which to create the Wine Pub. The size of the room will be about 100 square meters, in order to guarantee the necessary space for musical performances and the reception of customers.

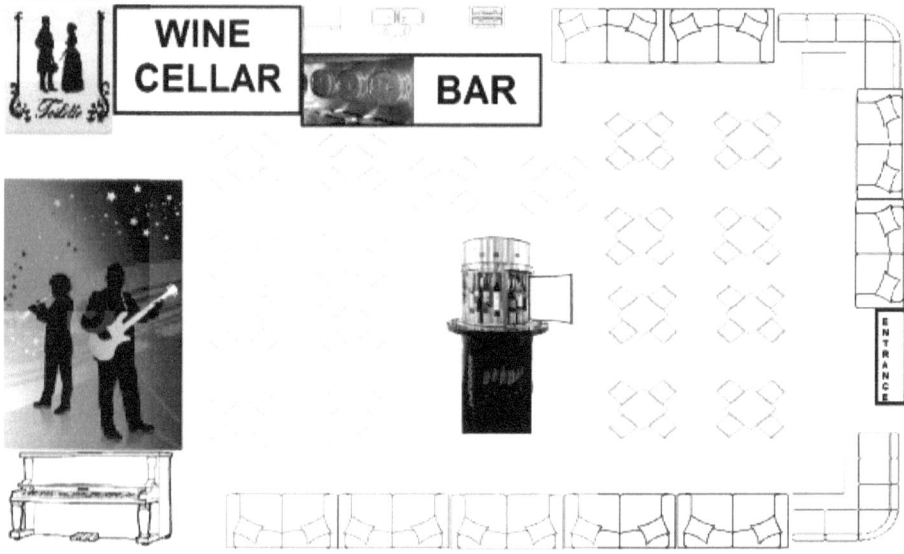

Figure 14: Hypothetical layout of my Wine Pub according to my own elaboration

The characterizing element of this type of layout is to have everything in one room, from the bar, to the live music area, tables and sofas. In this way is encouraged the socialization among customers, a difficult thing if there were small rooms. With this type of layout, even the lone customer is encouraged to join in the Wine Pub and sit where he likes.

The capacity of the Wine Pub, considering a room of 100 square meters with the space occupied by the furniture, the toilet, the live music area, the bar and the wine cellar, can hold up to a maximum of 60 people, excluding staff.

9.2 TOOLS

The tools within the Wine Pub distinguish itself from the other wine bars and pubs. In particular, the dispensing system of bulk wine and the Enomatic system make my Wine Pub unique.

Figure 15: Drink System srl in Vinovo (TO), Italy, produces the system of tapping bulk wine
http://www.drinksystem.it/real.asp?IDCat=Vino

As already mentioned (chapter 5 Mission), in these dispensing systems of bulk wine directly from the demijohns, already installed in Italy in different wine bars, tapping takes place via pneumatic pumps actuated by compressed air. In demijohns, pressure is compensated with the use of Nitrogen for food use.

The system described above is only an example; it is possible to customize the type of system at will.

Drink System srl, an Italian company located in Vinovo near Turin, produced the system in the picture above. This tool gives the possibility to tap wine as if it was beer. In addition, there is the ability to import in Ireland directly bulk wine at lower prices compared to that sold bottled.

Figure 16: Impianto Botte produced by Celli SpA in San Giovanni in Marignano (RN), Italy
http://www.celli.com/products/impianto-botte_297.html

Drink System srl collaborates with Celli SpA, another Italian firm located in San Giovanni in Marignano near Rimini, which produces a system for dispensing wine called "Impianto Botte" that can contain 8 liters of wine to be placed above the bar.

In Ireland, it is possible to buy the products of Celli SpA through the distributor MLH Holding Ltd located in Coolmine Dublin.

Another important tool, discovered by analyzing the main competitors of Cork, Arthur Mayne, is the Enomatic system. Unlike the one installed in the wall at Arthur Mayne, the model I am interested in is cylindrical, to be placed in the middle of the Wine Pub.

Figure 17: Enomatic system produced by Enomatic srl http:// www.enomatic.it/new/default.asp?catIDPadre=33&catID=34&NewsLan=ENG

The model "enoround" in the above figure can hold 16 bottles. By inserting a prepaid card, customers can select the wine required by using an LCD touch screen display.

Enomatic srl is an Italian company located in Strada in Chianti near Florence. The distributor for Ireland is located in Norwich, UK.

9.3 FURNITURE

The furnishings of my Wine Pub will have the style of the classic Irish Pub but among the accessories, there will be something of Italian origin. The size of the room, about 100 square meters, greatly influences the type of design. What absolutely cannot miss is the presence of high stools to drink wine directly at the bar, tables and chairs for those who want to eat something to accompany the wine, and finally comfortable sofas for those who want to relax while enjoying the live music. The important thing is to figure out the size of the furniture, leaving no gaps or spaces too tight to move.

The style of wood will be alternated with leather sofas. The walls will be decorated with paintings of various Italian towns, and on each table, there will be a candle to create the right atmosphere. When customers enter the Wine Pub will be impressed with the decor similar to that of an Irish Pub, but with details typically Italian. Nothing is left to chance; every piece of furniture will be placed in the appropriate place to make my Wine Pub unique.

A potential supplier of furniture could be Cork Bar Furniture[79]. This company produces furniture for Irish pubs, hotels and restaurants since 1923. Their showroom is located in Ballygarvan, two miles from Cork Airport.

Figure 18: Products of Cork Bar Furniture

The menu will consist of various types of Italian wines from different regions and some cold dishes to match.

White wines

- <u>Pinot Grigio</u> (Veneto): this is the typical aperitif wine, to be consumed during happy hour or paired with fresh cheeses and salads.
- <u>Chardonnay</u> (Veneto): This is a very famous wine in France, produced also in Italy, and it is often consumed during aperitif or with a dessert.

Sparkling white wines

- <u>Spumante dolce</u> (Piemonte): Wine for special occasions to serve to serve with fruit salads, desserts, panettone or pandoro.
- <u>Spumante secco</u> (Veneto): Wine for aperitifs and appetizers.

Red wines

- <u>Primitivo</u> (Puglia): This typical wine from Puglia is combined with spicy salami and spicy cheeses.
- <u>Montepulciano d'Abruzzo</u> (Abruzzo): This is a wine from the center of Italy to associate with mature cheeses such as pecorino accompanied by mushrooms.
- <u>Barolo</u> (Piemonte): Italian wine famous all over the world combines well the Parmigiano Reggiano and Grana Padano accompanied by truffles, or you can consume it with chocolate desserts.
- <u>Negramaro</u> (Puglia): Ancient wine of Salento, you can

drink it with all kinds of dishes, especially combines well with seasoned cured meats and sheep cheeses.

- <u>Sangiovese</u> (Emilia Romagna): Typical wine of Romagna combines with starters of salami and Parmesan cheese.
- <u>Pinot nero</u> (Lombardia): Wine of French origin, but also produced in Italy, joins well to speck ham and smoked cheeses.
- <u>Barbera</u> (Lombardia): Wine to accompany meats, semi-hard cheeses and mushrooms.
- <u>Dolcetto</u> (Piemonte): Wine of friendship and companionship, suitable for matching with salami and cheese.
- <u>Nero d'Avola</u> (Sicilia): Wine tasting deep to combine with spicy fish dishes.

Sparkling red wines

- <u>Lambrusco</u> (Emilia Romagna): Light wine to drink in combination with bacon, salami, mortadella, Parmigiano Reggiano and Grana Padano.

Cold dishes

- <u>Appetizers for aperitif</u>: different types of finger food to be enjoyed alone or with friends and it is recommended to associate with a glass of white wine or dry sparkling white wine.
- <u>Bread with spicy salami and spicy provolone cheese</u>: it is recommended to associate with a glass of red wine type Primitivo.
- <u>Bread with ham, goat cheese and mushrooms</u>: it is recommended to associate with a glass of red wine type Montepulciano d'Abruzzo or Negramaro or Barbera.
- <u>Bread with Parma ham, Parmesan and truffles</u>: it is recommended to associate with a glass of red wine type Barolo.
- <u>Bread with salami and Parmesan cheese</u>: it is recommended to associate with a glass of red wine type

Sangiovese or Dolcetto.

- <u>Bread with speck ham and smoked cheese</u>: it is recommended to associate with a glass of red wine type Pinot Nero.
- <u>Grilled tuna with lemon sauce accompanied by black olives and cherry tomatoes</u>: it is recommended to associate a glass of red wine type Nero d'Avola.
- <u>Buffalo mozzarella with Parma ham and cherry tomatoes</u>: it is recommended to associate a glass of red wine type Montepulciano d'Abruzzo.

Desserts

- <u>Fruit salad</u>: it is recommended pairing with a glass of sparkling white wine type Spumante dolce.
- <u>Pannacotta</u>: it is recommended pairing with a glass of sparkling white wine type Spumante dolce.
- <u>Tiramisù</u>: it is recommended pairing with a glass of sparkling white wine type Spumante dolce.

9.5 ENTERTAINMENT

Entertainment is the most interesting part of my Wine Pub. It will be the main reason why people will enter the Wine Pub. Everything will take place in a small stage where there will be a piano and the space needed for the performances. Each day will perform different artists, with whom I'll hold lasting partnerships. There will be performances of classical music, jazz, blues, rock, modern music, some typical local dance, etc.

Most artists will be unknown and the Wine Pub is an opportunity for them to be known by the people of Cork. The recruitment of the artists will take place along the streets of Cork, where they already perform occasionally. The idea is to bring artists from performing in the street to my Wine Pub.

PART 3

Operative section

10. MARKETING PLAN

Having defined widely in section 7 who is the target customer and thoroughly analyzed the market, the time has come to expose which marketing strategies to be taken to promote the Wine Pub.

In this chapter will be defined which marketing materials to use to promote my Wine Pub, such as a website, brochures and flyers. Then will be analyzed some promotion strategies to be implemented to reach new customers. Some tactics are television spots, newspaper articles, magazines and online advertising, special events to be organized in the Wine Pub.

Like it or not, today it is increasingly important to be present online, since customers before going to a pub or bar, consult the website, read online reviews and they want to be informed of all the services offered. Therefore, it is essential to have a good online marketing strategy. In particular, I must identify the keywords to find the website in various search engines, update the website constantly, pay online advertising, exploiting all existing social media.

10.1 MARKETING MATERIALS

L isted below are the various marketing materials that are to be used to promote the Wine Pub and methods to use them:

Flyers: Flyers keep potential customers' eyes on the Wine Pub. The distribution of flyers in the streets is crucial in the two weeks before the opening, just to notify the population of the opening of the Wine Pub in their city. Then, the distribution will take place every time in the week prior to a special event organized in the Wine Pub.

Postcards: This marketing solution is through the mail. Postcards will be sent to all those customers who purchase prepaid cards of the Enomatic system. In the postcards, there will be special offers throughout the year.

Brochures: Great way to tell the story of the Wine Pub are the tri-fold brochures to be distributed each month in all the hotels and bed and breakfast in Cork. The hotels in Cork put at their entrance a desk with all the brochures of the various pubs, restaurants and attractions of the city to be consulted by their guests. Inside the brochure will be the wine menu, address, opening hours and a description of the Wine Pub.

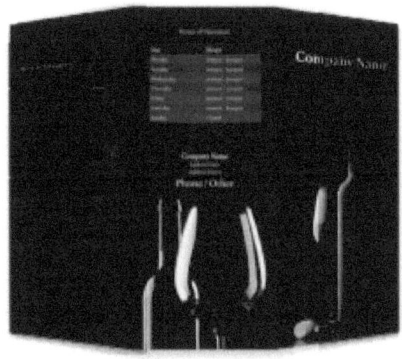 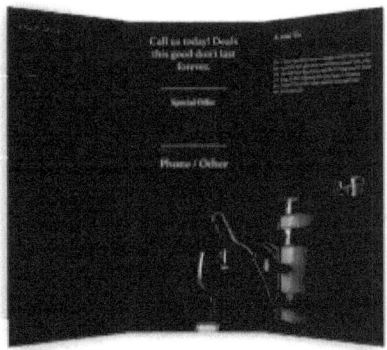

Figure 1919: Example of a tri-fold brochure created by Vitasprint
http://www.vistaprint.com/?no_redirect=1 &xnav=logo

Paper coasters: Reusable coasters to use inside the Wine Pub to keep the logo in sight.

Corporate gifts: At Christmas, Epiphany and Easter, the Wine Pub will give to all its customers some bottle openers.

Business cards: To be left to everyone I meet, the business cards contain information to contact me.

Calendars: Everybody likes calendars. The last day of the year will be given away to all guests of the Wine Pub, calendars depicting images of wines and vineyards with a brief description of their quality.

Website: The website will have on his homepage a brief description of the Wine Pub and a calendar updated daily with the list of all the artists who will perform during the week. There will be a page in which will be described in more detail the Wine Pub with pictures and videos. In yet another page, there will be a menu of wines and food.

10.2 PROMOTIONS STRATEGY

This paragraph is the most important within my marketing plan and explains in detail how to reach new customers. There are many promotional tactics; below there are some promotional tactics to be taken to reach the target customer.

Radio ads: Radio is a tool of mass communication very effective on the local area. Many people listen to local radio in the car, at home and at work. The most popular radio in Cork is Cork's RedFM[80], so it is of utmost importance to be present with radio spots on that radio during the evening hours.

Press ads: It is also important to be present with advertising on local newspapers. The most popular newspaper in Cork is Cork Independent[81], freely distributed throughout the city.

Online advertising: Fundamental is the website, which must be visible on computers, tablets, smartphones and smart TV. Particularly important is being on Google Map to be found by customers and on TripAdvisor[82] trying to get the best reviews. Having the company page on Facebook is another way to improve visibility online. Develop an application for smartphones and tablets to keep up with the times and promote the Wine Pub.

Events sponsorship: During the year, the city of Cork is full of events, festivals, sports events, music, and cultural activities. To improve the visibility of the Wine Pub is necessary to sponsor the most popular events such as the Cork Jazz Festival in October, the Cork Film Festival in November, the celebration of Christmas in December, the St. Patrick's Day Festival on March 17, the marathon in June, etc.[83]

10.3 ONLINE MARKETING STRATEGY

This section focuses on everything that is possible to do to promote the Wine Pub online. As explained previously, it is essential to have a website and be present on social media like Facebook.

The website will be constantly updated on the home page where there will be a calendar of events in the program and on the other pages with photographs and videos of past events with a brief description of them. Will be shown not only images of musicians but also the wine consumed in the Wine Pub. This is a way to show what happens inside the Wine Pub to potential customers and to revive moments of joy to existing customers.

Once the website has been created, I must have a specific keyword strategy to get more visibility as possible. Having the right combination of keywords can make the difference on search engines like Google. The keywords should be closely related with the type of business, in this case the Wine Pub. The keywords chosen are as follows: Wine Pub, wine, pub, Cork, music, entertainment, fun, relax, food, Italian, quality, made in Italy.

With the keywords chosen is possible to use as a tool for online marketing strategy "Pay Per Click Advertising". This tool allows viewing the website each time a user types keywords in the search engine. With this system, I pay a fee to the search engine each time a user clicks on the ad link. In the first few months, to get better visibility, it is essential to use Google AdWords[84].

Consumers will have the ability to communicate with the Wine Pub directly via their smartphone by connecting on Facebook, leaving comments and sending messages. The strategy to be adopted is to listen to the customers constantly and in real time, take part in their conversation and engage them to take part in various activities of the Wine Pub.

11. TECHNICAL-PRODUCTION PLAN

This section specify which activities will be undertaken to develop the Wine Pub based on the guidelines already mentioned in Chapter 9. In addition, I will analyze in detail the equipment used, highlighting the costs, time and manner of performing the activity in the Wine Pub and sources of supply.

11.1 CREATION OF THE WINE PUB

To begin to realize the Wine Bar, I need the right building in the right place. To find the right building I can consult two websites, MyHome[85] and Daft[86], which collect most of the real estate listings of the various agencies in Ireland. I can also visit the Allsop[87] website where there are ads of real estate sold at auction.

Keeping the parameters already identified in Chapter 9, which is a premise of approximately 100 square meters located in Cork city center, I can find properties for sale or rent in various prices. Regarding the purchase of the property there are prices ranging from € 1,000 up to € 5,000 per square meter. This means that premises of 100 square meters in Cork city center can cost from € 100,000 to € 500,000. The price variation depends on the state of the property. Cheap properties are often divided into several floors and in need of a complete renovation. The most expensive properties are in good condition and already used for pub or restaurant. The alternative is to rent an empty premise for about € 20,000 per year. This means having limits in setting the Wine Pub and every improvement made to the building is to the benefit of the landlord. Another alternative is to purchase a leasehold right. In this case, I will have to pay an amount that is between € 30,000 up to € 50,000 for the leasehold right to the leaseholder seller and the annual rent as per contract.

The building selected for the opening of the Wine Pub may require a restructuring. It becomes difficult to know what I am going to spend on a restructuring without having a quote of an architect. Fortunately, the technology helps me and now it is possible to estimate how much it might cost to renovate a building with automatic calculators offered by some websites. Obviously, since it is a calculator very rough, the figures must be treated as hypothesis. Through one of the websites available, I calculated how much it might cost to renovate a building of 100 square meters, built with standard materials and finishes, with significant variations of the floor plan layout, equal to 50%, with a new electrical system and standard air heating. I suggested the replacing of seven doors, replacement of nine windows, new parquet floor for 45 square meters, new single-fired floor for 35 square meters, new bathroom of 13 square meters, painting for 300 square meters. The estimate of the renovation is about 92,000 €[88].

As for the furniture, I personally visited the showroom of Cork Bar Furniture. They only produce tables, chairs, stools and sofas as shown in figure 18 in section 9.3. Assuming a premise of 100 square meters, I could buy from them 40 chairs model Hants to match with 20 tables model Sidney, five couches model Elle 2 Seater and 10 stools model Burbank.

As for the kitchen, there is the company Cork Bar & Catering Equipment Ltd, located near Cork Airport, which handles the installation of everything need in the kitchen. They also have a catalog of second hand equipment[89].

For kitchen accessories, next to Cork Bar & Catering Equipment there is the wholesaler Musgrave. In the large store of Musgraves, it is possible to buy clothes for chefs, cutlery, glasses, plates and pans.[90]

Bag in Box

Once I found the suitable place where to create the Wine Pub, it comes time to choose which types of systems to install for dispensing bulk wine. As mentioned in paragraph 9.2, in Italy there are many Italian companies that produce such equipment, including Drink System srl and Celli SpA.

In choosing the type of system, it is important to note that the various equipment can tap wine from different containers such as demijohns, kegs and bag in box. Particularly important considering that wine has to travel from Italy to Ireland.

The demijohns and kegs, once empty, have to go back to be washed, disinfected and re-bottled. This involves a double cost of transport and consumption of water, detergents, electricity, and labor for washing. The most convenient way is to use the bag in box.

The bag in box is a container for liquid foods made of plastic, enclosed in a cardboard box and equipped with a valve for emptying. The valve prevents air to penetrate into the plastic bag during emptying in order to preserve the wine contained. The bag in box is easy to carry and store, when empty it is thrown in the rubbish bins

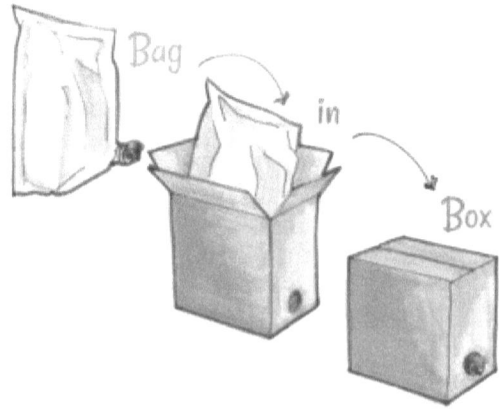

Figure 20: Bag in box, source: http://www.vinicartasegna.it/ vino-in-bag-in-box-praticita-qualita/

Vintar snc

An Italian company that manufactures tapping bulk wine from bag in box is Vintar snc, located in Corato near Bari. The system model that interests me is barrel-shaped and has an integrated cooling system. It can hold two 20-liter bag-in-box and provides wine from a tap column.

Figure 21: Barrel for dispensing bulk wine BF8OLC model produced by Vintar snc http://www.vintar.it/ita/BF8OLC.html

Getting in touch via email with Vintar snc, I could know more information about the system shown in Figure 21. The model with a column of dispensing costs € 2300 + VAT, while the two-way dispensing costs € 2700 + VAT. As payment if sold abroad, Vintar snc requires a bank transfer of 100% of the price and it is VAT-free. Shipping costs are to be quantified according to the destination and the model chosen. The system is installed by connecting the plug to a socket.

Celli SpA

The system of tapping bulk wine called "Impianto Botte", already shown in figure 16 in section 9.2, produced by Celli SpA, can be customized to draw wine from the bag in box. Since I came into contact via email with Celli SpA, which very kindly sent me the technical details of the system, I was able to view the various types of possible installations.

As can be seen from the technical details in the appendix, the system is formed by a barrel-shaped outer body (Exhibit I) in which there are electronic components (Exhibit II) connected to a coolant tank (Exhibit III). The system of tapping bulk wine, then, is connected to the bag in box with a tube that passes under the bar (Exhibit IV).

Casolo Ginelli Giorgio

An artisan, Mr. Casolo Ginelli Giorgio, resident in Somma Lombardo near Varese, produces systems of tapping bulk wine from the bag in box very similar to those of Vintar snc, Drink System srl and Celli SpA. Unlike the others, he puts on his website[91] the price, excluding VAT, of such systems. The plant barrel-shaped costs 715 € + VAT while the system mounted on a wooden panel with four taps it costs € 1490 + VAT.

Figure 22: Dispensing systems bulk wine from bag in box manufactured by Mr. Casolo Ginelli Giorgio

Enomatic srl

As for the Enoround system already shown in Figure 17 of paragraph 9.2, produced by Enomatic srl, it is possible to download the technical sheet directly from their website[92]. Appendix shows the technical drawing.

Enoround has a cylindrical shape and can hold up to 16 bottles of wine from which pull out the wine. There are two versions, the 16 bottles in one compartment or the version 8 + 8 bottles divided into two compartments (Exhibit V). It can refrigerate the wine from 7 to 18 degrees Celsius. In the version with two compartments, it is possible to have two different temperatures in order to split the white wines from red wines. The system works in a self-service way and can serve two clients at a time through the insertion of a prepaid card in one of two readers available. Customers can select the type and the quantity of wine through an LCD touch screen (Exhibit VI). The system uses nitrogen to maintain the flavor of the wine (Exhibit VII).

By contacting the sales office of Enomatic srl for Northern Europe, located in Norwich (UK), I could see that the purchase price of the Enoround Elite (base included) and software Card Generator 2.0 costs £18,495.00 + £3,699.00 (20% VAT) for a total of £22,194.00. Converted into Euros at the exchange rate of 0.7487 €/£ dated October 13, 2015 corresponds to € 24,702.82 + € 4,940.56 (20% VAT) = € 29,643.38. Pricing includes transport, installation and training.

Enomatic srl offers a 24-month warranty on all components. As payment terms, Enomatic srl require 50% to confirm the order and the rest before the date of installation. Card Generator 2.0 software requires a Windows 7 operating system or newer, 2 GB of RAM, 2 GB HDD and a USB port for the card reader.

Showine

For the realization of the wine cellar, in Porto Mantovano near Mantova there is Showine[93], an Italian company specialized in creating customized wine cellars. For Showine it is important that the wine will be served at the right temperature in order to taste the quality of the wine. For this reason, they realize refrigerated wine cellar and refrigerator showcases for display.

Among the products of Showine, what interests me most are the cold rooms for wine storage. In this cold storage, it is possible to store the wine in bottles and bag in boxes. The cold storage rooms of Showine are easy to assemble and connect to an electrical outlet. The capacity of cold storage rooms for wine ranges from 600 bottles of 0.75 liters up to 4140 bottles of 0.75 liters. Therefore can be stored from 450 liters of wine up to 3105 liters depending on the size of the refrigerator. Prices of cold storage rooms range from € 5,980 for the 600 bottles cold room, up to 24,000 € for the 4140 bottles one. Sizes range from H 2,05m x L 1,27m x W 1.17m for the cold storage of 600 bottles, up to H 2,05m x L 1,87m x W 4,35m for the cold storage of 4140 bottles. The choice of the size of the cabin fridge will depend on the floor plan of the property of the Wine Pub.

Figure 23: Cabina clima 4140 produced by Showine
http://www.showine.it/cabina-clima-4140.html

11.2 RUNNING THE WINE PUB

After completing the creation of the Wine Pub, the next step is to make it work. To do that I need products to sell, that is the Italian wine and food, staff, artists, electricity, water and gas.

Wine

"La Cantina di Giorgio" of Casolo Ginelli Giorgio in Somma Lombardo (VA) has a large price list of wines in Bag in Box[94]. As can be read from his website, a pack of 20 liters of Pinot Grigio in Bag in Box is sold at € 36.00, therefore 1.80 €/l. Pinot Nero is sold at € 34.00, therefore 1.70 €/l. Like him there are many other wineries selling wine in Bag in Box from which to supply. In Bag in Box, it is possible only to buy still wines. Sparkling wines have to be bottled.

After selecting the suppliers, I have to transport the wine from Italy to Ireland. Supposing to carry 500 liters of wine, through an automatic calculator available on the websites of some shippers is possible to calculate how much it costs to transport 500 liters of wine from Italy to Ireland:

- FedEx[95], the cost is € 1,907.50 with a transit time of one week.
- Global Service[96], the cost is € 1,396.40 with a transit time of one week.
- TNT[97], the cost is € 1,838.82 with a transit time of one week.

This means having a shipping cost per liter ranging between € 2.80 up to € 3.80 depending on the chosen shipper. Besides the cost of transport, I must be aware of the excise duty on wine.

As can be seen by consulting the tables of excise duties on alcoholic beverages published by the European Commission[98] in Ireland for a still wine with an alcohol content between 5.5% to 15% is applied an excise duty of € 424.84 per hectolitre. If the alcohol content exceeds 15% is applied an excise duty of € 616.45 per hectolitre. For sparkling wines with alcohol content over than 5.5% will apply an excise duty of € 849.68 per hectolitre. For all wines with an alcohol content lower than or equal to 5.5% applies an excise duty of € 141.57. In addition, I also have to consider that in Ireland the VAT on wine is 23%.

In summary, if I wanted to know how much it costs per liter to import in Ireland from Italy wine Pinot Grigio in a pack of 20 liters Bag in Box I should add the cost of the wine bought from "La Cantina di Giorgio", therefore € 1.80 per liter. Then, the cost of transport with the shipper Global Service, which for a lot of 500 liters, the cost per liter is about € 2.80, then I have to add the excise duty for a still wine with alcohol content between 5.5% and 15%, therefore € 424.84 per hectolitre, thus € 4.84 per liter. The sum of € 1.80 + € 2.80 + € 4.84 = € 9.44 per liter. Not including the 23% VAT.

Food

As for Italian food, I can buy directly in Cork by "The Boot's Specialities"[99], company owned by an Italian family that since about ten years has a wholesale and retail of Italian products located near Cork Airport.

Figure 24: The Boot's Specialities warehouse, Unit 21
City Link Park, Forge Hill, Kinsale Rd., Cork, Ireland

Gas & Electricity

As regards the supply of gas and electricity, in Ireland there are various alternatives. Via the Bonkers website[100] is possible to compare various offers of different companies. Through the website, it is possible to compare the combined prices of Gas & Electricity, Electricity only or Gas only. In my case, I selected Gas & Electricity. Prices have been estimated based on the national average electricity consumption (5,300kWh) and national average gas consumption (13,800kWh); the Commission for Energy Regulation provides this information.

For a place located in an urban area without electricity Night Saver meter, without a previous natural gas supply, paying by direct debit, an annual contract prices vary between € 1,008.10 and € 1,206.16 per year. Prices vary by the type of company and the features of the contract. For each type of contract are specified the details.

Water

A state company provides water supply in Ireland[101]. The fare is calculated according to consumption, equivalent to € 1.85 per cubic meter (1,000 liters) for water supplied and € 1.85 per cubic meter (1,000 liters) for wastewater removed.

Staff

After creating the Wine Pub and have the material resources to make it work, it is time to mention the staff. The staff is the most important element of the entire Wine Pub. Without staff, the Wine Pub would be useless. Considering that the Wine Pub would have a size of 100 square meters, with a bar and a lounge with tables, to provide good service to customers, there must be 6 to 7 people working simultaneously.

The staff will be organized in this way: a person will be working at the cash register; one person will be cooking in the kitchen, two people will stand at the bar, and two or three waiters will serve the tables in the lounge.

The Wine Pub will be open to the public from 16:00 to 2:00 during the week, except on Saturday that the closure will be at 3:00. The staff will have to start the service an hour before the opening and ending one hour after closing. During the hour before the opening, the staff will take care of all the activities necessary to prepare the Wine Pub to welcome customers. During the time after closing, the staff will take care of the cleaning.

The shifts will be of 6 hours throughout the week, except for those who will work on Saturday night that will have a 7-hour shift. The first shift is from 15:00 to 21:00. The second shift will be from 21:00 to 3:00 during the week, except Saturday night that the shift will end at 4:00. To cover the busiest time range, the third waiter will have a shift from 18:00 to 24:00.

The staff who work at the cash register, in the kitchen and at the bar, will be trained so that they can be interchanged in case a staff member were missing for any reason. If were missing a waiter, one of the two working at the bar will have to replace him.

Considering that six people work in the first shift for 6 hours 7 days a week, the number of hours a week to pay for the first shift is 6 x 6 x 7 = 252 hours worked. Another six people working in the second shift for 6 hours 6 days a week, plus seven hours on Saturday night, the number of hours a week to pay for the second shift is 6 x 6 x 6 + 6 x 7 = 258 hours worked. Finally, the third shift of the waiter for 6 hours 7 days a week, therefore 6 x 7 = 42 hours worked. The sum of all the hours of work that must be paid in one week is 252 + 258 + 42 = 552 hours worked.

Now the minimum wage in Ireland is € 8.65 per hour, but from 2016 will be increased to € 9.15[102]. Since the opening of the Wine Pub will take place after 2016, the cost of the salary will be calculated on € 9.15 per hour. Therefore, 552 hours a week multiplied for € 9.15 is equal to € 5.050,80 a week. In Ireland, wages are paid weekly.

The number of employees varies according to the performance of the business. If revenues are not sufficient to cover all costs, I will have to reduce the number of staff. Conversely, if customers are more than expected and as a result, revenues more than expected, I will increase the staff.

Artists

Musicians, singers and dancers will be recruited on the streets of Cork, along Oliver Plunkett Street and St. Patrick Street, where they already perform daily. To them will be offered employment contracts for the occasional night when they will perform. The amount of those benefits will vary according to the artist. Generally, for a street artist, remuneration does not exceed 100 €.

12. ORGANIZATIONAL PLAN

I will own the 100% of the company. Maria Theresa Adams and I will compose the management. Our profiles are fully described in chapter 6. I will take care mainly of the administration and everything related to the back office, while Maria will be responsible for the operational part in the Wine Pub.

The key operational roles needed are:

Chef: the ideal person must know how to prepare simple Italian dishes, must have a significant experience in the job, a willingness to work in a team, good organizational skills, creative spirit and attention to quality and detail.

Barman: the ideal person must know the main Italian wines.

Waiter: the ideal person has experience in the job, good communication skills, ability to customer contact, physical appearance cured.

Cashier: the ideal person must have a short experience in the job knowing the use of the cash register and the use of the POS for credit cards.

The figure below depicts the organizational chart. The artists and the accountant are independent from the Wine Pub, but they closely cooperate with it. The chef, the barman, waiters and the cashier receive directions directly from Maria. She will be responsible for recruitment, being in close contact with the staff. I will take care of the strategic planning and management control.

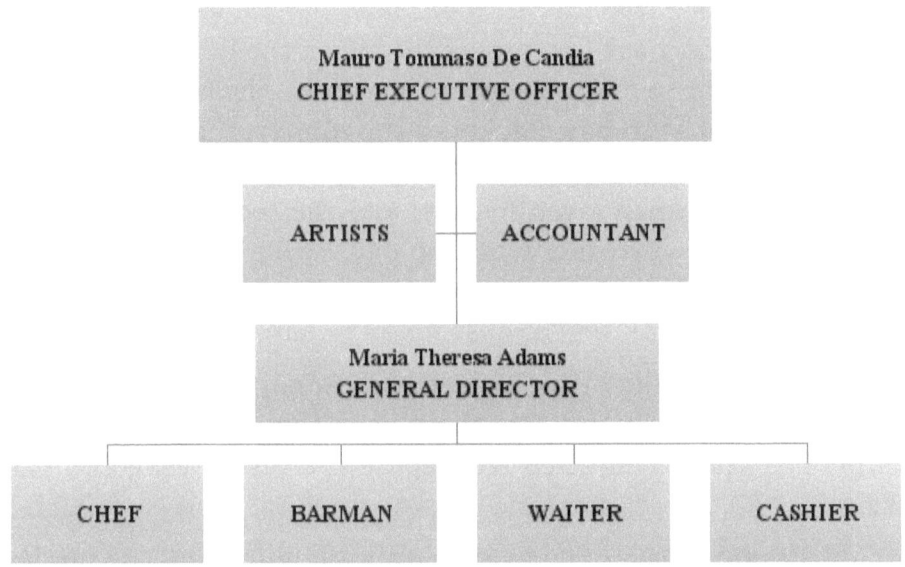

Figure 25:Organization chart

The organizational process of the Wine Pub is the following.

At the entrance of the Wine Pub, customers will have the option to sit at a table, go and sit at the bar stool or sit on a couch. Waiters are required to go to both customers at the tables and those on the sofas to take orders. After the order, the waiter has to go by the chef and barman and ask them to prepare food and wine glasses. Then, the waiter has to give glasses of wine and food to customers. After that the customer finish to consume, the waiter has to ask the customer if he wants anything else of if he wants the bill. If the customer wants something else, the waiter take another order, if the customer wants the bill, the waiter has to go to cashier to take the bill and bring it back to the customer.

Pocketed the money, the waiter goes to the cashier to give him the money and to take the rest to bring back to the customer. If the customer wants to pay by card, the waiter goes to get the mobile POS and returns the customer to make the payment.

The barman must ask customers sitting on the bar stools which wine they want to order. Received the order, the barman should ask the customer to pay. Pocketed the money, the barman goes to the cashier to give him the money and to get the rest and the receipt. The barman gives the rest and the receipt back to the customer. If the customer wants to pay with a card, the barman brings the mobile POS to the customer and make the payment. Finally, the barman serves the customer the wine ordered.

The cashier is obliged to collect the money from customers, waiters and barman and give them back the change and the receipt. The chef is required to prepare the dishes asked by the waiter.

As for the repurchase of wine from Italy, knowing that the carrier takes a week to deliver the wine, I will have to keep a threshold of reordering that ensures coverage of one week and three days for possible delays. Therefore, when the remaining wine in the wine cellar will be sufficient for ten days, I reorder the wine. The amount of wine ordered will be the wine lacking to fill the wine cellar and the wine that will be consumed during the week of delivery. Italian food can be purchased daily from the importer in Cork.

13. ECONOMIC-FINANCIAL PLAN

F inally came the time to sum up everything that has been written previously. In this chapter, there will be sales budget, purchasing budget, income statement and a balance sheet for the first three years of business. However, before making any such budget, I have to do an investments budget in order to know how much I will have to invest to start the Wine Pub.

As mentioned in paragraph 11.1, for the choice of the property of 100 square meters in Cork city center where to start the business, there are several alternatives:

1) Building in bad condition sold at a price of € 100,000; cost of the restructuring € 92,000. Total amount: € 100,000 + € 92,000 = € 192,000.

2) Building in poor condition sold at a price of € 300,000; cost of the restructuring is 50% of the total renovation, therefore € 92,000 x 50% = € 46,000. Total amount: € 300,000 + € 46,000 = € 346,000.

3) Building in good condition sold at a price of € 500,000; no cost of restructuring. Total expenditure: € 500,000.

4) Building in poor condition rented at a price of € 20,000 per year; restructuring costs equal to 50% of total renovation, therefore € 46,000. Total amount: € 46,000 + € 20,000 per year.

5) Building in good condition rented at a price of € 20,000 per year; the leaseholder sells his leasehold right for € 40,000. Total amount: € 40,000 + € 20,000 per year.

I choose the number one because is the most affordable and I can make all the changes I want to the property. In the building chosen, I should install the Vintar barrel for dispensing two-bulk wine BF80LC model: € 2,700; Mr. Casolo Ginelli Giorgio's dispensing systems four bulk wine: € 1,490; Enomatic Enoround: € 24,703; Showine Cabina Clima 2040 bottles: €14,100. The total installations is given by € 2,700 + € 1,490 + € 24,703 €14,100 = € 42,993.

The value of the land, not depreciable, is equal to 20% of the property, then € 38 400. The depreciation of the property equal to 3% per year, will be calculated on € 192,000 - € 38,400 = € 153,600. Therefore, the annual depreciation is € 4,608. The installations are depreciated by 12% annually. Therefore the annual depreciation is € 42,993 x 12% = € 5,159. The furniture is € 20,000, depreciated by 10% annually. Catering equipment (crockery, cutlery, and kitchen equipment) is € 5,000, depreciated by 25% annually.

The table below shows the investment budget in the first three years of operation.

Investment budget 31/12/2019		Initial value	Depreciation	Final value
Building	Historical value	192,000		192,000
	Depreciation fund	0	4,608	4,608
Installations	Historical value	42,993		42,993
	Depreciation fund	0	5,159	5,159
Furniture	Historical value	20,000		20,000
	Depreciation fund	0	2,000	2,000
Catering equipment	Historical value	5,000		5,000
	Depreciation fund	0	1,250	1,250
Investment budget 31/12/2020		Initial value	Depreciation	Final value
Building	Historical value	192,000		192,000
	Depreciation fund	4,608	4,608	9,216
Installations	Historical value	42,993		42,993
	Depreciation fund	5,159	5,159	10,318
Furniture	Historical value	20,000		20,000
	Depreciation fund	2,000	2,000	4,000
Catering equipment	Historical value	5,000		5,000
	Depreciation fund	1,250	1,250	2,500
Investment budget 31/12/2021		Initial value	Depreciation	Final value
Building	Historical value	192,000		192,000

	Depreciation fund	9,216	4,608	13,824
Installations	Historical value	42,993		42,993
	Depreciation fund	10,318	5,159	15,477
Furniture	Historical value	20,000		20,000
	Depreciation fund	4,000	2,000	6,000
Catering equipment	Historical value	5,000		5,000
	Depreciation fund	2,500	1,250	3,750

I decide to buy the property with a twenty-year mortgage with a fixed monthly payment of € 639.62 and fixed interest rate to 5.24%. The bank finances 95% of the property value, therefore € 95,000.00. The repayment of the mortgage for the first three years is as follows[103]:

Mortgage repayment schedule				
Deadline	Residual capital	Mortgage payments	Interests	Capital
Jan – 19	95,000.00	-	-	-
Feb – 19	94,775.21	639.62	414.83	224.79
Mar – 19	94,549.44	639.62	413.85	225.77
Apr – 19	94,322.69	639.62	412.87	226.76
May – 19	94,094.94	639.62	411.88	227.75
Jun – 19	93,866.20	639.62	410.88	228.74
Jul – 19	93,636.46	639.62	409.88	229.74
Aug – 19	93,405.72	639.62	408.88	230.74
Sep – 19	93,173.97	639.62	407.87	231.75
Oct – 19	92,941.21	639.62	406.86	232.76
Nov – 19	92,707.43	639.62	405.84	233.78
Dec – 19	92,472.63	639.62	404.82	234.80
Jan – 20	92,236.81	639.62	403.80	235.82
Feb – 20	91,999.95	639.62	402.77	236.85
Mar – 20	91,762.07	639.62	401.73	237.89
Apr – 20	91,523.14	639.62	400.69	238.93
May – 20	91,283.17	639.62	399.65	239.97
Jun – 20	91,042.15	639.62	398.60	241.02
Jul – 20	90,800.08	639.62	397.55	242.07
Aug – 20	90,556.95	639.62	396.49	243.13
Sep - 20	90,312.76	639.62	395.43	244.19
Oct – 20	90,067.51	639.62	394.37	245.26
Nov – 20	89,821,18	639.62	393.29	246.33
Dec – 20	89,573.78	639.62	392.22	247.40
Jan – 21	89,325.30	639.62	391.14	248.48
Feb – 21	89,075.73	639.62	390.05	249.57
Mar – 21	88,825.07	639.62	388.96	250.66
Apr – 21	88,573.32	639.62	387.87	251.75
May – 21	88,320.47	639.62	386.77	252.85

Jun – 21	88,066.51		639.62	385.67	253.96
Jul – 21	87,811.45		639.62	384.56	255.06
Aug – 21	87,555.27		639.62	383.44	256.18
Sep – 21	87,297.97		639.62	382.32	257.30
Oct – 21	87,039.55		639.62	381.20	258.42
Nov – 21	86,780.00		639.62	380.07	259.55
Dec – 21	86,519.32		639.62	378.94	260.68

Now, I have to figure out how many glasses of wine will be sold in the Wine Pub per day. Knowing that the Wine Pub opens to the public at 16 pm and closes at 2:00 am (Saturday at 3:00 am) and that the maximum occupancy is 60 people, the calculation is represented in the following table:

2019 Week	Mon	Tue	Wed	Thu	Fri	Sat	Sun	Total
16:00-17:00	5	6	7	8	9	10	9	54
17:00-18:00	10	12	14	16	18	20	18	108
18:00-19:00	15	18	21	24	27	30	27	162
19:00-20:00	20	24	28	32	36	40	36	216
20:00-21:00	25	30	35	40	45	50	45	270
21:00-22:00	30	36	42	48	54	60	54	324
22:00-23:00	25	30	35	40	45	50	45	270
23:00-24:00	20	24	28	32	36	40	36	216
00:00-01:00	15	18	21	24	27	30	27	162
01:00-02:00	10	12	14	16	18	20	18	108
02:00-03:00						10		10
Total	175	210	245	280	315	360	315	1,900
2020 Week	Mon	Tue	Wed	Thu	Fri	Sat	Sun	Total
16:00-17:00	5	6	7	8	9	10	10	55
17:00-18:00	10	12	14	16	18	20	20	110
18:00-19:00	15	18	21	24	27	30	30	165
19:00-20:00	20	24	28	32	36	40	40	220
20:00-21:00	25	30	35	40	45	50	50	275
21:00-22:00	30	36	42	48	54	60	60	330
22:00-23:00	25	30	35	40	45	50	50	275
23:00-24:00	20	24	28	32	36	40	40	220
00:00-01:00	15	18	21	24	27	30	30	165

01:00-02:00	10	12	14	16	18	20	20	110
02:00-03:00						10		10
Total	**175**	**210**	**245**	**280**	**315**	**360**	**350**	**1,935**
2021 Week	**Mon**	**Tue**	**Wed**	**Thu**	**Fri**	**Sat**	**Sun**	**Total**
16:00-17:00	5	6	7	8	10	10	10	56
17:00-18:00	10	12	14	16	20	20	20	112
18:00-19:00	15	18	21	24	30	30	30	168
19:00-20:00	20	24	28	32	40	40	40	224
20:00-21:00	25	30	35	40	50	50	50	280
21:00-22:00	30	36	42	48	60	60	60	336
22:00-23:00	25	30	35	40	50	50	50	280
23:00-24:00	20	24	28	32	40	40	40	224
00:00-01:00	15	18	21	24	30	30	30	168
01:00-02:00	10	12	14	16	20	20	20	112
02:00-03:00						10		10
Total	**175**	**210**	**245**	**280**	**350**	**360**	**350**	**1,970**

The table shows that in 2019 will be sold in the Wine Pub about 1,900 glasses of wine per week, in 2020 about 1935 glasses per week, finally in 2021 approximately 1,970 glasses per week. Considering that in a year there are 52 weeks, means serving 1,900 x 52 = 98,800 glasses of wine in 2019, 1935 x 52 = 100,620 glasses in 2020, 1970 x 52 = 102,440 glasses in 2021. Assuming that each of them glasses of wine has a size of 200 ml, i.e. 1/5 liter, meaning that in 2019 will be sold 98,800/5 = 19,760 liters of wine in 2020 will be sold 100,620/5 = 20,124 liters of wine and in 2021 will be sold 102,440/5 = 20,488 liters of wine.

In the following pages, there are tables with the sales budget of 2019, 2020 and 2021. The amounts of wine are in liters. Wine prices are per liter. Food prices are for single dish.

Sales Budget 2019			
Menu	Quantity	Price	Total
White wines			
Pinot Grigio	6,400	25.00	160,000.00
Chardonnay	6,246	25.00	156,150.00
Total white wines	12,646		**316,150.00**
Sparkling white wines			
Spumante dolce	1,600	40.00	64,000.00
Spumante secco	1,562	60.00	93,720.00
Total sparkling white wines	3,162		**157,720.00**
Red wines			
Primitivo	350	30.00	10,500.00
Montepulciano d'Abruzzo	360	30.00	10,800.00
Barolo	340	50.00	17,000.00
Negramaro	370	30.00	11,100.00
Sangiovese	320	35.00	11,200.00
Pinot nero	380	35.00	13,300.00
Barbera	310	40.00	12,400.00
Dolcetto	390	35.00	13,650.00
Nero d'Avola	342	35.00	11,970.00
Total red wines	3,162		**111,920.00**
Sparkling red wines			
Lambrusco	790	35.00	27,650.00
Total sparkling red wines	790		**27,650.00**
Cold dishes			
Appetizers	990	11.00	10,890.00
Bread, spicy salami, provolone	1,000	12.00	12,000.00
Bread, ham, goat cheese, mushroom	980	14.00	13,720.00
Bread, Parma ham, Parmesan, truffles	1,010	14.00	14,140.00

Bread, salami, Parmesan	970	12.00	11,640.00
Bread, speck ham, smoked cheese	1,020	12.00	12,240.00
Grilled tuna, black olives, cherry tomatoes	960	14.00	13,440.00
Buffalo mozzarella, Parma ham, cherry tomatoes	974	23.00	22,402.00
Total cold dishes	7,904		**110,472.00**
Desserts			
Fruit salad	660	8.00	5,280.00
Pannacotta	640	9.00	5,760.00
Tiramisù	676	9.00	6,084.00
Total desserts	1,976		**17,124.00**
Total revenues			**741,036.00**

Sales Budget 2020			
Menu	Quantity	Price	Total
White wines			
Pinot Grigio	6,500	25.00	162,500.00
Chardonnay	6,379	25.00	159,475.00
Total white wines	12,879		**321,975.00**
Sparkling white wines			
Spumante dolce	1,700	40.00	68,000.00
Spumante secco	1,520	60.00	91,200.00
Total sparkling white wines	3,220		**159,200.00**
Red wines			
Primitivo	360	30.00	10,800.00
Montepulciano d'Abruzzo	370	30.00	11,100.00
Barolo	350	50.00	17,500.00
Negramaro	380	30.00	11,400.00
Sangiovese	330	35.00	11,550.00
Pinot nero	390	35.00	13,650.00
Barbera	320	40.00	12,800.00
Dolcetto	400	35.00	14,000.00
Nero d'Avola	320	35.00	11,200.00
Total red wines	3,220		**114,000.00**
Sparkling red wines			
Lambrusco	805	35.00	28,175.00
Total sparkling red wines	805		**28,175.00**
Cold dishes			
Appetizers	1,000	11.00	11,000.00
Bread, spicy salami, provolone	1,100	12.00	13,200.00
Bread, ham, goat cheese, mushroom	990	14.00	13,860.00
Bread, Parma ham, Parmesan, truffles	1,110	14.00	15,540.00

Bread, salami, Parmesan	980	12.00	11,760.00
Bread, speck ham, smoked cheese	1,120	12.00	13,440.00
Grilled tuna, black olives, cherry tomatoes	970	14.00	13,580.00
Buffalo mozzarella, Parma ham, cherry tomatoes	780	23.00	17,940.00
Total cold dishes	8,050		**110,320.00**
Desserts			
Fruit salad	670	8.00	5,360.00
Pannacotta	650	9.00	5,850.00
Tiramisù	692	9.00	6,228.00
Total desserts	2,012		**17,438.00**
Total revenues			**751,108.00**

Sales Budget 2021			
Menu	**Quantity**	**Price**	**Total**
White wines			
Pinot Grigio	6,600	25.00	165,000.00
Chardonnay	6,512	25.00	162,800.00
Total white wines	13,112		**327,800.00**
Sparkling white wines			
Spumante dolce	1,700	40.00	68,000.00
Spumante secco	1,578	60.00	94,680.00
Total sparkling white wines	3,278		**162,680.00**
Red wines			
Primitivo	370	30.00	11,100.00
Montepulciano d'Abruzzo	380	30.00	11,400.00
Barolo	360	50.00	18,000.00
Negramaro	390	30.00	11,700.00
Sangiovese	340	35.00	11,900.00
Pinot nero	400	35.00	14,000.00
Barbera	330	40.00	13,200.00
Dolcetto	410	35.00	14,350.00
Nero d'Avola	298	35.00	10,430.00
Total red wines	3,278		**116,080.00**
Sparkling red wines			
Lambrusco	820	35.00	28,700.00
Total sparkling red wines	820		**28,700.00**
Cold dishes			
Appetizers	1,100	11.00	12,100.00
Bread, spicy salami, provolone	1,200	12.00	14,400.00
Bread, ham, goat cheese, mushroom	1,000	14.00	14,000.00
Bread, Parma ham, Parmesan, truffles	1,120	14.00	15,680.00

Bread, salami, Parmesan	990	12.00	11,880.00
Bread, speck ham, smoked cheese	1,130	12.00	13,560.00
Grilled tuna, black olives, cherry tomatoes	980	14.00	13,720.00
Buffalo mozzarella, Parma ham, cherry tomatoes	675	23.00	15,525.00
Total cold dishes	8,195		**110,865.00**
Desserts			
Fruit salad	690	8.00	5,520.00
Pannacotta	660	9.00	5,940.00
Tiramisù	699	9.00	6,291.00
Total desserts	2,049		**17,751.00**
Total revenues			**763,876.00**

As for the inventories, I must make a distinction between that for wines and that for the food. Inventories of the wines are limited by the capacity of the Wine Cellar, which in this case is equivalent to a capacity of 2040 bottles of 0.75 liters, then 1530 liters of wine. As explained in Chapter 12, knowing that the carrier takes a week to transport wine from Italy to Ireland, the reorder level should be equal to a supply of wine of one week and three days for any delays, therefore 10 days.

Knowing also that in one week of 2019 are consumed 1900 glasses of wine of 200 ml, then 380 liters of wine per week, or about 54 liters of wine per day (380/7), the reorder level will be equal to 54 liters x 10 days = 540 liters of wine. This means that when in the wine cellar there are only 540 liters of wine left, I have to order more wine. The wine to be ordered must be equal to the amount missing to fill the Wine Cellar, and then 1530 - 540 = 990 liters, and the amount of wine consumed during the shipping, so 990 + 380 = 1370 liters of wine. This means that every time in the Wine Cellar there are only 540 liters of wine left, I order 1,370 liters of wine. Knowing also that each day are consumed 54 liters of wine, I can calculate how many days I have to order the wine. Since the capacity of the Wine Cellar less the stock for the reordering is equal to 990 liters, the wine must be re-ordered every 18 days (990/54). In a year, I will have to order the wine about 20 times (365/18).

As for the food, however, being easily perishable products and of short duration, the purchase of such goods must take place every day. The amount to be purchased is the one necessary to fill the re-frigerator of the Wine Pub.

Below are tables of purchasing budget for the years 2019, 2020 and 2021. The quantities purchased correspond with the quantities sold in order to keep inventories unchanged. The purchase price of the wine is 50% of the sale price. In this price it is included the cost of transport and excise duties. Purchase prices of food is 80% of the sale price.

Purchasing Budget 2019			
Menu	Quantity	Price	Total
White wines			
Pinot Grigio	6,400	12.50	80,000.00
Chardonnay	6,246	12.50	78,075.00
Total white wines	12,646		**158,075.00**
Sparkling white wines			
Spumante dolce	1,600	20.00	32,000.00
Spumante secco	1,562	30.00	46,860.00
Total sparkling white wines	3,162		**78,860.00**
Red wines			
Primitivo	350	15.00	5,250.00
Montepulciano d'Abruzzo	360	15.00	5,400.00
Barolo	340	25.00	8,500.00
Negramaro	370	15.00	5,550.00
Sangiovese	320	17.50	5,600.00
Pinot nero	380	17.50	6,650.00
Barbera	310	20.00	6,200.00
Dolcetto	390	17.50	6,825.00
Nero d'Avola	342	17.50	5,985.00
Total red wines	3,162		**55,960.00**
Sparkling red wines			
Lambrusco	790	17.50	13,825.00
Total sparkling red wines	790		**13,825.00**
Cold dishes			
Appetizers	990	8.80	8,712.00
Bread, spicy salami, provolone	1,000	9.60	9,600.00
Bread, ham, goat cheese, mushroom	980	11.20	10,976.00
Bread, Parma ham, Parmesan, truffles	1,010	11.20	11,312.00

Bread, salami, Parmesan	970	9.60	9,312.00
Bread, speck ham, smoked cheese	1,020	9.60	9,792.00
Grilled tuna, black olives, cherry tomatoes	960	11.20	10,752.00
Buffalo mozzarella, Parma ham, cherry tomatoes	974	18.40	17,921.60
Total cold dishes	7,904		**88,377.60**
Desserts			
Fruit salad	660	6.40	4,224.00
Pannacotta	640	7.20	4,608.00
Tiramisù	676	7.20	4,867.20
Total desserts	1,976		**13,699.20**
Total purchasing cost			**408,796.80**

Purchasing Budget 2020			
Menu	Quantity	Price	Total
White wines			
Pinot Grigio	6,500	12.50	81,250.00
Chardonnay	6,379	12.50	79,737.50
Total white wines	12,879		**160,987.50**
Sparkling white wines			
Spumante dolce	1,700	20.00	34,000.00
Spumante secco	1,520	30.00	45,600.00
Total sparkling white wines	3,220		**79,600.00**
Red wines			
Primitivo	360	15.00	5,400.00
Montepulciano d'Abruzzo	370	15.00	5,550.00
Barolo	350	25.00	8,750.00
Negramaro	380	15.00	5,700.00
Sangiovese	330	17.50	5,775.00
Pinot nero	390	17.50	6,825.00
Barbera	320	20.00	6,400.00
Dolcetto	400	17.50	7,000.00
Nero d'Avola	320	17.50	5,600.00
Total red wines	3,220		**57,000.00**
Sparkling red wines			
Lambrusco	805	17.50	14,087.50
Total sparkling red wines	805		**14,087.50**
Cold dishes			
Appetizers	1,000	8.80	8,800.00
Bread, spicy salami, provolone	1,100	9.60	10,560.00
Bread, ham, goat cheese, mushroom	990	11.20	11,088.00
Bread, Parma ham, Parmesan, truffles	1,110	11.20	12,432.00

Bread, salami, Parmesan	980	9.60	9,408.00
Bread, speck ham, smoked cheese	1,120	9.60	10,752.00
Grilled tuna, black olives, cherry tomatoes	970	11.20	10,864.00
Buffalo mozzarella, Parma ham, cherry tomatoes	780	18.40	14,352.00
Total cold dishes	8,050		**88,256.00**
Desserts			
Fruit salad	670	6.40	4,288.00
Pannacotta	650	7.20	4,680.00
Tiramisù	692	7.20	4,982.40
Total desserts	2,012		**13,950.40**
Total purchasing cost			**413,881.00**

Purchasing Budget 2021			
Menu	Quantity	Price	Total
White wines			
Pinot Grigio	6,600	12.50	82,500.00
Chardonnay	6,512	12.50	81,400.00
Total white wines	13,112		**163,900.00**
Sparkling white wines			
Spumante dolce	1,700	20.00	34,000.00
Spumante secco	1,578	30.00	47,340.00
Total sparkling white wines	3,278		**81,340.00**
Red wines			
Primitivo	370	15.00	5,550.00
Montepulciano d'Abruzzo	380	15.00	5,700.00
Barolo	360	25.00	9,000.00
Negramaro	390	15.00	5,850.00
Sangiovese	340	17.50	5,950.00
Pinot nero	400	17.50	7,000.00
Barbera	330	20.00	6,600.00
Dolcetto	410	17.50	7,175.00
Nero d'Avola	298	17.50	5,215.00
Total red wines	3,278		**58,040.00**
Sparkling red wines			
Lambrusco	820	17.50	14,350.00
Total sparkling red wines	820		**14,350.00**
Cold dishes			
Appetizers	1,100	8.80	9,680.00
Bread, spicy salami, provolone	1,200	9.60	11,520.00
Bread, ham, goat cheese, mushroom	1,000	11.20	11,200.00
Bread, Parma ham, Parmesan, truffles	1,120	11.20	12,544.00

Bread, salami, Parmesan	990	9.60	9,504.00
Bread, speck ham, smoked cheese	1,130	9.60	10,848.00
Grilled tuna, black olives, cherry tomatoes	980	11.20	10,976.00
Buffalo mozzarella, Parma ham, cherry tomatoes	675	18.40	12,420.00
Total cold dishes	8,195		**88,692.00**
Desserts			
Fruit salad	690	6.40	4,416.00
Pannacotta	660	7.20	4,752.00
Tiramisù	699	7.20	5,032.80
Total desserts	2,049		**14,200.80**
Total purchasing cost			**420,522.80**

For measuring inventories of wine, i.e. 1,530 liters stored in the Wine Cellar, as they are all different wines with different prices, I have to calculate the weighted average price of a liter of wine. Prices refer to the cost of purchase.

The calculation for the year 2019 is the following: 306,720.00/19,760 = € 15.52 per liter.

Therefore, 15.52 x 1,530 = € 23,745.60 (wine inventories 2019).

The calculation for the year 2020 is the following: 311,675.00/20,124 = € 15.49 per liter.

Therefore, 15.49 x 1,530 = € 23,699.70 (wine inventories 2020).

The calculation for the year 2021 is the following: 317,630.00/20,488 = € 15.50 per liter.

Therefore, 15.50 x 1,530 = € 23,715.00 (wine inventories 2021).

As for food supplies, since they are purchased daily and stored in the refrigerator with a stock of one day, the value of inventories of food will be given by the total price of all food purchased during the year divided by 365 days. In this way, I can know the value of food purchased in a day corresponding to that in the refrigerator.

For the year 2019, the value of food inventories is 102,076.80/365 = € 279.66;

For the year 2020, the value of food inventories is 102,206.40/365 = € 280.02;

For the year 2021, the value of food inventories is 102,892.80/365 = € 281.90.

As for the cost of the staff, as I had already calculated in section 11.2, the weekly paychecks are € 5,050.80. This means that in one year the salaries are € 5,050.80 x 52 weeks = € 262,641.60. Another cost to keep in mind is the performance of the artists. If I want to have an artist every day and pay him € 100 per day, in a year I will spend € 36,500.00. For accounting, the payroll of the employees, tax returns and financial statements, the accountant's fee estimated amounts to € 7,000.00 per year.

To implement the marketing plan of Chapter 10, I decided to spend € 10,000.00 per year. The Gas & Electricity bill, as estimated in paragraph 11.2, will be annually about € 1.206.16. In addition, I estimate a water bill equal to € 500.00 per year. Financial expenses in 2019 are € 4,508.46, in 2020 are € 4,776.59, and in 2021 are € 4,620.99. In the following table, the budget of the operating costs.

Operating costs budget	2019	2020	2021
Purchase of goods	408,796.80	413,881.00	420,522.80
Change in inventories	0.00	45.90	-15.30
Salaries	262,641.00	262,641.00	262,641.00
Artists performances	36,500.00	36,500.00	36,500.00
Accountant's fee	7,000.00	7,000.00	7,000.00
Marketing expenses	10,000.00	10,000.00	10,000.00
Gas & Electricity bill	1,206.00	1,206.00	1,206.00
Water bill	500.00	500.00	500.00
Total operating costs	726,643.80	731,773.90	738,354.50

Below the income statement.

Income statement	2019	2020	2021
Revenues	741,036.00	751,108.00	763,876.00
Operating costs	-726,643.80	-731,773.90	-738,354.50
EBITDA	14,392.20	19,334.10	25,521.50
Depreciations	-13,017.00	-13,017.00	-13,017.00
EBIT	1,375.20	6,317.10	12,504.50
Financial expenses	-4,508.46	-4,776.59	-4,620.99
EBT	-3,133.26	1,540.51	7,883.51
Tax	0	-385.13	-1,970.88
Net result	-3,133.26	1,155.38	5,912.63

Below the balance sheet.

Assets	2019	2020	2021	Liabilities	2019	2020	2021
Tangible assets	246,976	233,959	220,942	Mortgages	92,472	89,573	86,519
Inventories	23,746	23,700	23,715	Equity	200,000	196,867	197,791
Cash	18,617	29,936	45,797	Reserves	0	0	231
				Net result	-3,133	1,155	5,913
Tot assets	289,339	287,595	290,454	Tot liabil.	289,339	287,595	290,454

The loss of 2019 will be covered with a reduction in equity. The profit for 2020 will be allocated 20% to reserve, the rest goes to increase the equity. The profit for 2021 will be allocated 20% to reserve, the remaining part will be distributed.

ROE (2019) = (-3,133)/200,000 x 100 = -1.57%

ROI (2019) = 14,392/289,339 x 100 = 4.97%

ROE (2020) = 1,155/196,867 x 100 = 0.59%

ROI (2020) = 19,334/287,595 x 100 = 6.72%

ROE (2021) = 5,913/198,022 x 100 = 2.99%

ROI (2021) = 25,522/290,454 x 100 = 8.79%

As stated in the income statement, in the first year of operation the Wine Pub will record a loss. The loss is due to financial charges. In fact, the ROI of 2019 is 4.97%. In the following years, thanks to increased ROI, the Wine Pub will go into profit up to have a return on equity in 2021 amounted to 2.99%.

14. LAW AND REGULATIONS

Before starting a business in Ireland, I must obtain a Personal Public Service Number (PPS Number) in order to register for tax. The PPS Number is a personal identification number that is used to record all transactions with the government and the tax office. To get the PPS Number I have to go to the Department of Social Protection Office closer to me, in this case the Intreo Cork Centre in Hanover Street[104], and submit the following documents: passport, photo ID and proof of residence in Ireland like a household utility bill[105].

Then, I have to set a company and register it to the Companies Registration Office (CRO)[106]. In Ireland, there are various types of companies as laid down in the Companies Act 2014[107]. A brief description below:

LTD - Private Company Limited by Shares[108]: The responsibility of the shareholders in case of liquidation is limited to the value of the shares. The maximum number of members is 149 and there may be even just a director. An LTD may undertake any activities.

DAC - Designated Activity Company[109]: For this type of company, the Irish law makes two distinctions, one limited by shares and one limited by guarantee. In the company limited by shares, the shareholders are responsible only for the capital invested in the shares. In the company limited by guarantee, the shareholders are responsible for both the shares and a Fund for Guarantee, in the event of liquidation. The maximum number of members is 149 and there must be at least two directors. The constitution of a DAC includes a memorandum and articles of association.

PLC - Public Limited Company[110]: The liability of members is limited to the shares held. The nominal value of the company should not be less than € 25,000 and 25% of the share capital must be fully paid upon incorporation of the company.

CLG - Company Limited by Guarantee[111]: The responsibility of members in case of liquidation is limited to the amount contributed by them to the company as specified in the Memorandum. The company does not have a share capital owned by the members, so this type of company is primarily used by charitable organizations.

ULC - Private Unlimited Company; PUC - Public Unlimited Company; PULC - Public Unlimited Company that has no share capital[112]: In these three types of companies, shareholders are fully responsible with their personal assets for debts incurred by the company.

Among all types of companies listed above, I believe that the LTD is perfect for the Wine Pub. For setting up an LTD, the Companies Act 2014 provides for the drafting of a single document called the "articles of association"[113]. It is not necessary the memorandum and it is not necessary to write a stated object as a LTD can undertake all types of business.

During the formation of the company, I have to choose a company name. However, before choosing a company name I have to see through the "Company Search Facility"[114] if there is a company name similar or identical to that chosen. Before the establishment of the company, I can reserve the company name[115] for 28 days against payment of € 25.00 via the website of Companies Online Registration Environment (CORE)[116].

Every company has the obligation to display the name in a visible way out of the place where the activity is undertaken. In addition, the company name must appear on all official documents such as invoices, receipts, letters of credit, etc. In the website, letters, emails and faxes, in addition to the company name must indicated the legal form of the company, the location and the registration number, and the registered office address[117].

The address of the office to be registered to the CRO must be a physical location in order to be inspected. The activities of the Wine Pub to be declared to the CRO can be classified according to NACE Code[118] as "Food and beverage service activities". An LTD company can have one single director and a secretary who must be over 18[119].

Once drafted the articles of association of the company, the easiest way to register is to fill out an online form at the CORE website. The benefits of using the CORE website are that the certificate of incorporation will be issued in five days, no need to queue at the office desk and the commission is paid directly online by credit card.

After registering the company to the CRO, I must notify the local tax office. To make a tax return, calculate tax liability and pay, I have to use the Revenue On-Line Service (ROS)[120]. The Corporation Tax is calculated on profits and is divided into two rates: 12.5% for trading income and 25% for non-trading income.

15. CONCLUSION

Widespread opinion among the Italian wine producers is that nowadays the only path to follow to increase sales is internationalization. This is demonstrated by the statistical data in chapter 2 of Wine Monitor that show in fifteen years a negative trend in wine consumption in countries typically producers like Italy, France, Spain and Portugal, while an extraordinary increase by over 150% in countries such as Ireland, Czech Republic, Mexico and New Zealand.

Ireland is the country that fascinates me the most for its untouched nature and its friendly people. As explained in chapter 3, Ireland is an island politically divided in two jurisdictions that over the years has seen many wars of independence. The Irish people have suffered a famine in the mid-1800s, forcing a mass emigration to the United States. Became famous with the nickname Celtic Tiger for its incredible economic boom following the entry into the EEC in 1973. Ireland has also had an economic recession from 2008 to 2010. Over the past five years, the Irish economy is constantly growing.

Cork city, where I am going to start my business, is the second largest city in Ireland. As described in chapter 4, in the seventh century there was only a monastery, which became a Viking colony. Over the centuries, the city was occupied by the Normans and then by the British. Today, Cork is a city on a human scale and divided into four main areas: the city center, the north side, the south side and west side.

My mission, chapter 5, is to be able to convince the Irish people to appreciate the Italian wine by serving it on tap in a pub using a system of dispensing bulk wine. To accomplish this, my partner Maria Theresa Adams and I have to best use all our skills and knowledge. As explained in chapter 6, I can rely on a good preparation in business administration gained during my studies at the LIUC University. Maria Theresa Adams has the expertise to run the Wine Pub.

In order to succeed, it is important to identify who is the target customer. In Chapter 7, following a market survey conducted by me in the streets of Cork, where I was able to ask people of all ages and social groups to complete a questionnaire, I concluded that the target customer is a man about 40 years old who works in Cork city center. Obviously, different types of clients, men and women, workers, students, unemployed and retired people will come in the Wine Pub. Cork has a population of 123,000 inhabitants and alcoholism is very common, particularly among the unemployed.

Good knowledge of competitors, chapter 8, can be a source of inspiration and improvement. In fact, The Oliver Plunkett, a traditional Irish Pub in Cork with live music every night, inspires the Wine Pub. Another competitor, Arthur Mayne, made me discover the existence of the Enomatic system, an automatic dispensing wine from the bottle. To gain a competitive advantage, I have to focus on providing better service than the one offered by competitors.

The Wine Pub, chapter 9, will be located in downtown Cork and will have a size of about 100 square meters. Distinguishing features are the typical Irish pub style with Italian details. The tools used will be a system of tapping bulk wine and the Enomatic system positioned in the center of the Wine Pub. Furniture will be typical Irish, while food and the wine will be a typical Italian. The icing on the cake is a good entertainment of musicians and artists.

The activity of the Wine Pub will be accompanied by a good marketing plan, chapter 10, to promote it with flyers, brochures and a website. Important are advertising on the local radio, newspapers, online and events. A good web site full of pictures, videos, calendar events and contacts is an excellent showcase to be known internationally. Social media such as Facebook are a great tool to keep in touch with clients.

To realize the Wine Pub, chapter 11, first I have to find the right place. This involves constant monitoring of the real estate listings in Cork. Most likely, the premises chosen will require a restructuring. Then I will have to buy the equipment and furniture. As for the bulk wine dispensing equipment, I concluded that the most convenient format to draw the wine is from the Bag in Box. Several Italian companies, including Vintar snc and Celli SpA, realize these types of systems with different characteristics. Showine will implement the wine cellar. "La Cantina di Giorgio" in Somma Lombardo (VA) could be a potential supplier of wine in Bag in Box. I have to keep in mind that in addition to the cost of transport, Ireland applies excise duties on the import of wine. For Italian food, I can stock up from a local importer. Other facilities that I need will be water, gas and electricity.

The staff required, chapter 12, varies by a chef, a person at the cash register, two people at the bar and three waiters. Currently, the Irish law provides as minimum wage € 8.65 per hour that will be increased to € 9.15 in 2016.

The Economic-Financial Plan, chapter 13, shows an investment budget in three years and a mortgage repayment schedule assuming that I will be financed with bank loan € 95,000. There is also an estimate of the wine glasses sold at every hour during one week: In this way, I am able to calculate the liters of wine sold per week. Then there is a three-year sales budget based on estimates followed by a three-year purchasing budget. The income statement shows a slight loss in the first year mainly due to interest expense, followed by a profit of € 1,155 in the second year and € 5,912 in the third year. ROI in the first year is 4.97%, which means that despite the loss, the Wine Pub is able to cover all operating costs. In the next two years, ROI grows steadily until reaching

8.79% in the third year. Return on equity becomes positive in the second year and reaches 2.99% in the third year.

Among the various types of companies provided for by Irish law, chapter 14, I concluded that the one that fits better to the Wine Pub is LTD. This corporate form ensures me the limited liability, flexibility in the subject, and a reduced number of directors given that the minimum is one.

If the model of Wine Pub will work well and will be profitable, after the city of Cork will follow further openings in various cities of Ireland and maybe even in the rest of world. My dream is to create the "Starbucks" of wine.

Mauro Tommaso De Candia

REFERENCES

- Adams, E.; *How Catholic Ireland Became the First Country to Vote for Same-Sex "Marriage"*. National Catholic Register, May 26, 2015; https://www.ncregister.com/daily-news/how-catholic-ireland-became-the-first-country-to-vote-for-same-sex-marriage/
- Akhtar, S. I.; Jones, V. C.; *Proposed Transatlantic Trade and Investment Partnership (T-TIP): In Brief.* Congressional Research Service, June 11, 2014; https://www.fas.org/sgp/crs/row/R43158.pdf
- Bannon, M. J.; *Irish Urbanisation: Trends, Actions and Policy Challenges*. University College Dublin, May 2004; https://www.ucd.ie/gpep/research/workingpapers/2004/04-03.pdf
- Barry, F.; Bradley, J.; *FDI and Trade: the Irish host-country experience.* University College Dublin; http://www.tcd.ie/business/staff/fbarry/papers/papers/fdipapej.pdf
- Barry, F.; *Irish Economic Development over Three Decades of EU Membership.* University College Dublin, August 2003; http://www.tcd.ie/business/staff/fbarry/papers/papers/Finance%20a%20Uver.pdf
- Bohan, C.; *For the first time in seven years, Ireland's unemployment rate is under 10%.* thejournal.ie, May 21, 2015; http://www.thejournal.ie/irish-unemployment-rate-2115641-May2015/
- Buttolo, N.; *L'internazionalizzazione del mercato del vino tra crisi ed opportunità.* Fondazione CUOA, July 22, 2014; http://www.cuoaspace.it/2014/07/il-percorso-dellinternazionalizzazione-del-mercato-del-vino-tra-crisi-ed-opportunita.html
- CIA World Factbook website: https://www.cia.gov/library/publications/the-world-factbook/geos/ei.html

- *Companies Act 2014*: http://www.irishstatutebook.ie/eli/2014/act/38/enacted/en/pdf
- *Constitution of Ireland.* July 1, 1937; http://web.archive.org/web/20110721123409/http://www.constitution.ie/reports/ConstitutionofIreland.pdf
- *December 2014 CSO Livestock Survey*: http://www.cso.ie/en/releasesandpublications/er/lsd/livestocksurveydecember2014/#.VXcyeBuJhes
- Dell'Orefice, G.; *Sono export e innovazione le parole d'ordine del vino italiano.* Il Sole 24 Ore, April 3, 2013; http://www.ilsole24ore.com/art/impresa-e-territori/2013-04-03/sono-export-innovazione-parole-195809.shtml?uuid=AbhAn0jH
- Donnelly, J.; *The Irish Famine.* BBC, February 17, 2011; http://www.bbc.co.uk/history/british/victorians/famine_01.shtml
- *ECONOMIC POLICY REFORMS 2015: GOING FOR GROWTH.* OECD 2015, pag. 219-222; http://www.oecd.org/ireland/going-for-growth-ireland-2015.pdf
- Howley, M.; Holland M.; Dineen, D.; *Energy in Ireland.* SEAI, 2014; http://www.seai.ie/Publications/Statistics_Publications/Energy_in_Ireland/Energy_in_Ireland_Key_Statistics/Energy-in-Ireland-Key-Statistics-2014.pdf
- Kelly, T., Hayes, P.; *Cork City Profile 2014.* Cork City Council, 2014; http://www.hse.ie/eng/services/news/Cork_City_Profile.pdf
- Keough, M.; *Irish population could top pre-Famine levels - estimated to reach 6.7 million by 2046.* IrishCentral., May 3, 2013; http://www.irishcentral.com/news/irish-population-could-top-pre-famine-levels-estimated-to-reach-67-million-by-2046-206002691-237587091.html
- *Local Government Reform Act 2014.* June 2, 2014; http://www.environ.ie/en/LocalGovernment/LocalGovernmentAdministration/RHLegislation/FileDownLoad,35715,en.pdf

- *Low-tax policies created the Tiger*. Independent, October 24, 2004; http://www.independent.ie/opinion/editorial/lowtax-policies-created-the-tiger-26225791.html
- *Low Pay Commission recommends increase in National Minimum Wage of 50 cent to €9.15*. Department of Jobs, Enterprise and Innovation, 21st July 2015; https://www.djei.ie/en/News-And-Events/Department-News/2015/July/21072015.html
- McCloskey, J.; *Irish as a World Language*. University of Notre Dame, June 2006; http://ohlone.ucsc.edu/~jim/PDF/notre-dame.pdf
- McDonald, F.; *Turf-cutters defy EU law, say monitors*. The Irish Times, May 29, 2012; http://www.irishtimes.com/news/turf-cutters-defy-eu-law-say-monitors-1.524621
- Nolan, W.; *Geography of Ireland. Government of Ireland*, October 15, 2009; http://www.gov.ie/en/essays/geography.html
- *Northern Ireland Act 1998*; http://www.legislation.gov.uk/ukpga/1998/47/pdfs/ukpga_19980047_en.pdf
- O'Riordan, S.; *Cork County Council spends €10m on tourism promotion*. Irish Examiner, June 10, 2015; http://www.irishexaminer.com/ireland/cork-county-council-spends-10m-on-tourism-promotion-335566.html
- Shorto, R.; *The Irish Affliction*. The New York Times Magazine, February 9, 2011; http://www.nytimes.com/2011/02/13/magazine/13Irish-t.html?pagewanted=2&hpw&_r=0
- Smith, M. K.; *Expert's map shows 20 million redheads across Ireland and UK*. IrishCentral., August 27,2013; http://www.irishcentral.com/news/experts-map-shows-20-million-redheads-across-ireland-and-uk-221299751-237772471.html
- *Tourism Barometer*. Fáilte Ireland, May 2015; http://www.failteireland.ie/FailteIreland/media/WebsiteStructure/Documents/3_Research_Insights/3_General_SurveysReports/REPORT-Failte-Ireland-tourism-barometer-

May-2015.pdf?ext=.pdf

- *Trends in Irish tourism.* Jim Power Economics, February 2011; http://www.dublinport.ie/fileadmin/user_upload/documents/Tourism_prospects_report.pdf
- Whelan, K.; *Ireland's Economic Crisis. The Good, the Bad and the Ugly.* University College Dublin, July 2013; http://www.centralbank.gov.cy/media/pdf_gr/Ir_economic_crisis.pdf

APPENDIX

Exhibit I – Impianto Botte (Housing)

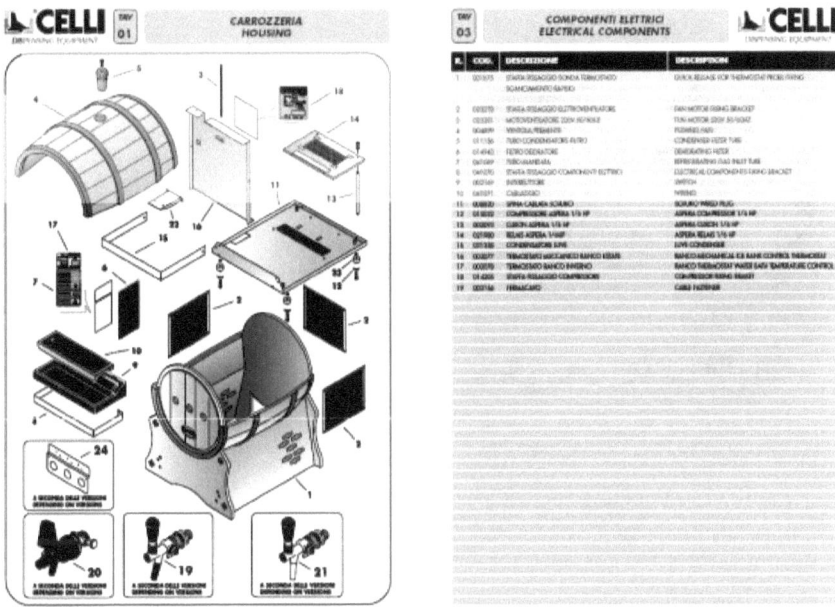

Figure 26: Impianto Botte produced by Celli SpA
in San Giovanni in Marignano (RN), Italy

Exhibit II – Impianto Botte (Electrical components)

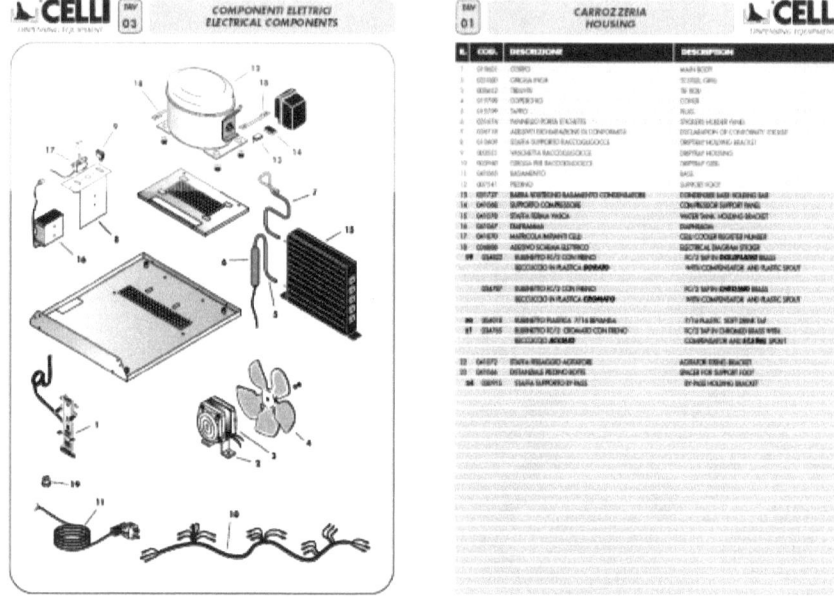

Figure 27: Impianto Botte produced by Celli SpA in San Giovanni in Marignano (RN), Italy

Exhibit III – Impianto Botte (Refrigerating water-tank)

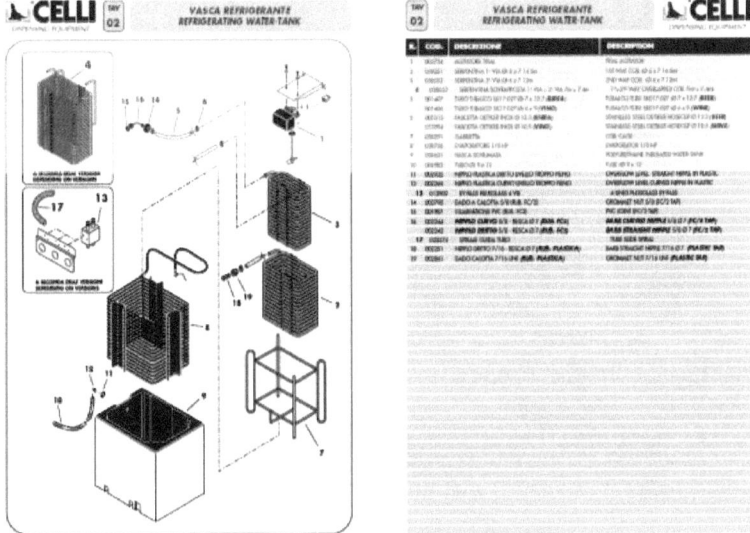

*Figure 28: Impianto Botte produced by Celli SpA
in San Giovanni in Marignano (RN), Italy*

Exhibit IV – Impianto Botte (Bag in Box)

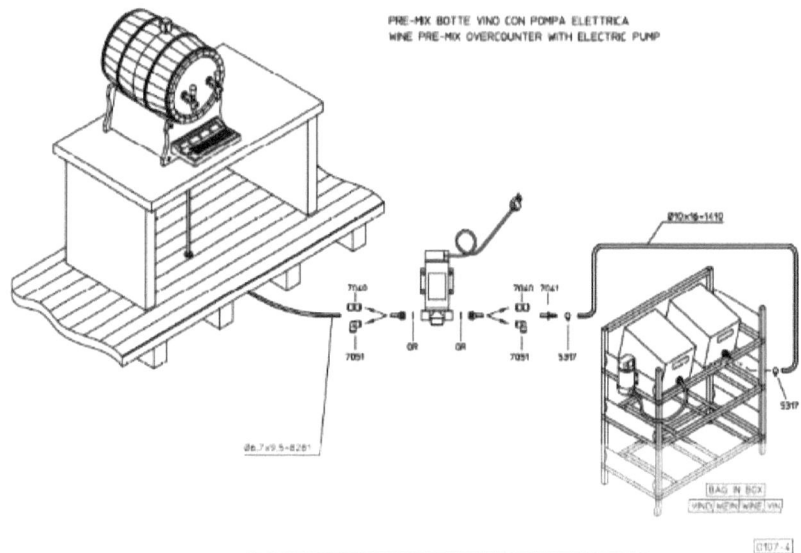

Figure 29: Impianto Botte produced by Celli SpA in San Giovanni in Marignano (RN), Italy

Exhibit V – Enoround (drawing 1)

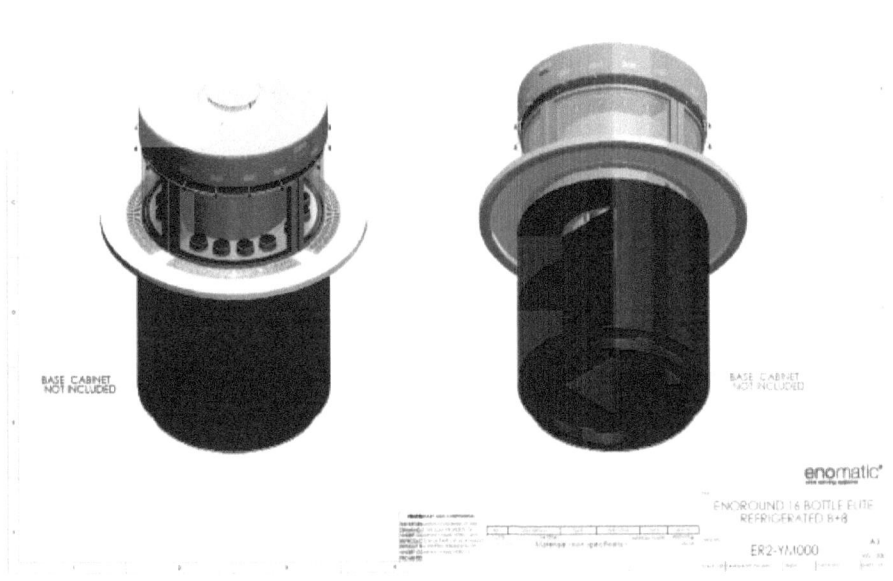

Figure 30: Enomatic system produced by Enomatic srl

Exhibit VI – Enoround (drawing 2)

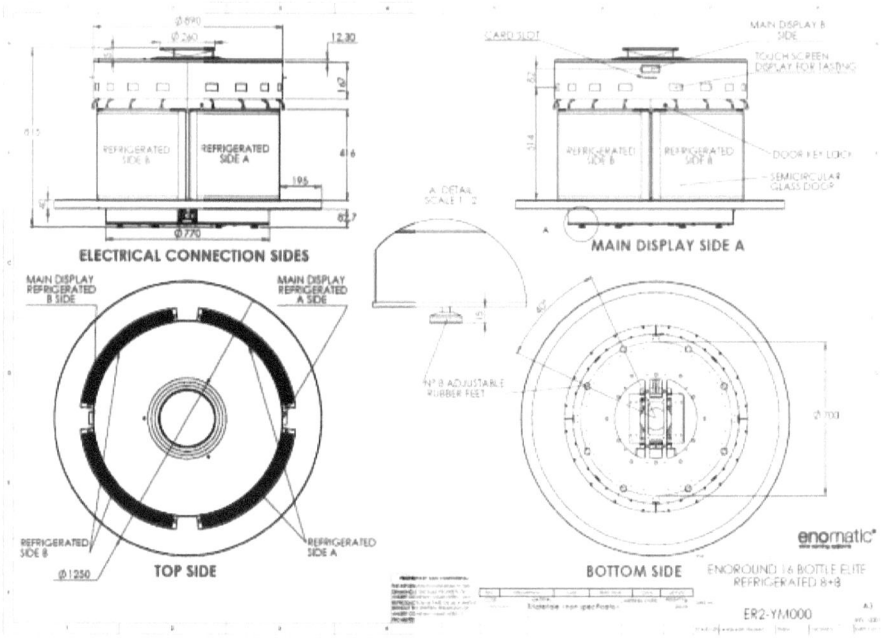

Figure 31: Enomatic system produced by Enomatic srl

Exhibit VII – Enoround (drawing 3)

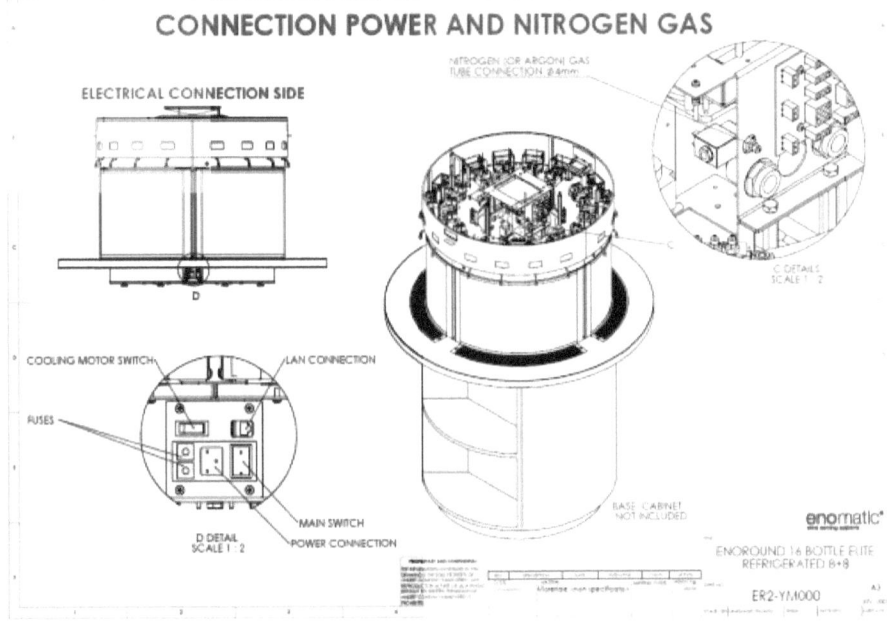

Figure 32: Enomatic system produced by Enomatic srl

[1] Nomisma website: http://www.nomisma.it/index.php/en/

[2] Wine Monitor website: http://www.winemonitor.it/en/

[3] Gruppo Italiano Vini website: http://www.gruppoitalianovini.com/index.php

[4] Casa Vinicola Zonin website: http://www.casavinicolazonin.it/

[5] Tenimenti Angelini website: http://www.tenimentiangelini.it/

[6] Consorzio di Tutela Vini DOC Sicilia website: http://www.consorziodocsicilia.it/

[7] Source: Dell'Orefice, G.; *Sono export e innovazione le parole d'ordine del vino italiano*. Il Sole 24 Ore, April 3, 2013; http://www.ilsole24ore.com/art/impresa-e-territori/2013-04-03/sono-export-innovazione-parole-195809.shtml?uuid=AbhAn0jH

[8] Source: Akhtar, S. I.; Jones, V. C.; *Proposed Transatlantic Trade and Investment Partnership (T-TIP): In Brief*. Congressional Research Service, June 11, 2014; https://www.fas.org/sgp/crs/row/R43158.pdf

[9] Source: Buttolo, N.; *L'internazionalizzazione del mercato del vino*

tra crisi ed opportunità. Fondazione CUOA, July 22, 2014; http://www.cuoaspace.it/2014/07/il-percorso-dellinternazionalizzazione-del-mercato-del-vino-tra-crisi-ed-opportunita.html

[10] Smith, M. K.; *Expert's map shows 20 million redheads across Ireland and UK.* IrishCentral., August 27,2013; http://www.irishcentral.com/news/experts-map-shows-20-million-redheads-across-ireland-and-uk-221299751-237772471.html

[11] Nolan, W.; *Geography of Ireland.* Government of Ireland, October 15, 2009; http://www.gov.ie/en/essays/geography.html

[12] The Irish Meteorological Service Online website: http://www.met.ie/default.asp

[13] Glenveagh National Park website: http://www.glenveaghnationalpark.ie/

[14] Ballycroy National Park website: http://www.ballycroynationalpark.ie/

[15] Connemara National Park website: http://www.connemaranationalpark.ie/

[16] Burren National Park website: http://www.burrennationalpark.ie/

[17] Killarney National Park website: http://www.killarneynationalpark.ie/

[18] Wicklow Mountains National Park website: http://www.wicklowmountainsnationalpark.ie/

[19] McDonald, F.; *Turf-cutters defy EU law, say monitors.* The Irish Times, May 29, 2012; http://www.irishtimes.com/news/turf-cutters-defy-eu-law-say-monitors-1.524621

[20] Donnelly, J.; *The Irish Famine.* BBC, February 17, 2011; http://www.bbc.co.uk/history/british/victorians/famine_01.shtml

[21] Keough, M.; *Irish population could top pre-Famine levels - estimated to reach 6.7 million by 2046.* IrishCentral., May 3, 2013; http://www.irishcentral.com/news/irish-population-could-top-pre-famine-levels-estimated-to-reach-67-million-by-2046-206002691-237587091.html

[22] Shorto, R.; *The Irish Affliction.* The New York Times Magazine, February 9, 2011; http://www.nytimes.com/2011/02/13/magazine/13Irish-t.html?pagewanted=2&hpw&_r=0

[23] Adams, E.; *How Catholic Ireland Became the First Country to Vote for Same-Sex "Marriage".* National Catholic Register, May 26, 2015; https://www.ncregister.com/daily-news/how-catholic-ireland-became-the-first-country-to-vote-for-same-sex-marriage/

[24] McCloskey, J.; *Irish as a World Language.* University of Notre Dame, June 2006; http://ohlone.ucsc.edu/~jim/PDF/notre-dame.pdf

[25] Bannon, M. J.; *Irish Urbanisation: Trends, Actions and Policy Challenges.* University College Dublin, May 2004; https://www.ucd.ie/gpep/research/workingpapers/2004/04-03.pdf

[26] Article 15.2 of the *Constitution of Ireland.* July 1, 1937; http://web.archive.org/web/20110721123409/http://www.constitution.ie/reports/

ConstitutionofIreland.pdf

[27] *Local Government Reform Act 2014*. June 2, 2014; http://www.environ.ie/en/LocalGovernment/LocalGovernmentAdministration/RHLegislation/FileDownLoad,35715,en.pdf

[28] *Northern Ireland Act 1998*; http://www.legislation.gov.uk/ukpga/1998/47/pdfs/ukpga_19980047_en.pdf

[29] Gaelic Athletic Association website: http://www.gaa.ie/

[30] Barry, F.; *Irish Economic Development over Three Decades of EU Membership*. University College Dublin, August 2003; http://www.tcd.ie/business/staff/fbarry/papers/papers/Finance%20a%20Uver.pdf

[31] *Low-tax policies created the Tiger*. Independent, October 24, 2004; http://www.independent.ie/opinion/editorial/lowtax-policies-created-the-tiger-26225791.html

[32] *ECONOMIC POLICY REFORMS 2015: GOING FOR GROWTH*. OECD 2015, pag. 219-222; http://www.oecd.org/ireland/going-for-growth-ireland-2015.pdf

[33] CIA World Factbook website: https://www.cia.gov/library/publications/the-world-factbook/geos/ei.html

[34] *Trends in Irish tourism*. Jim Power Economics, February 2011; http://www.dublinport.ie/fileadmin/user_upload/documents/Tourism_prospects_report.pdf

[35] *December 2014 CSO Livestock Survey*: http://www.cso.ie/en/releasesandpublications/er/lsd/livestocksurveydecember2014/#.VXcyeBuJhes

[36] Barry, F.; Bradley, J.; *FDI and Trade: the Irish host-country experience*. University College Dublin; http://www.tcd.ie/business/staff/fbarry/papers/papers/fdipapej.pdf

[37] Howley, M.; Holland M.; Dineen, D.; *Energy in Ireland*. SEAI, 2014; http://www.seai.ie/Publications/Statistics_Publications/Energy_in_Ireland/Energy_in_Ireland_Key_Statistics/Energy-in-Ireland-Key-Statistics-2014.pdf

[38] Whelan, K.; *Ireland's Economic Crisis. The Good, the Bad and the Ugly*. University College Dublin, July 2013; http://www.centralbank.gov.cy/media/pdf_gr/Ir_economic_crisis.pdf

[39] Cork city website: http://www.corkcity.ie/aboutcork/

[40] Jazz Festival website: http://www.guinnessjazzfestival.com/

[41] Cork Film Festival website: http://www.corkfilmfest.org/

[42] Cork city website: http://www.corkcity.ie/aboutcork/historyofcork/

[43] Cork Butter Museum website: http://www.corkbutter.museum/

[44] Crawford Art Gallery website: http://www.crawfordartgallery.ie/

[45] English Market website: http://www.englishmarket.ie/

[46] Cork City Gaol website: http://corkcitygaol.com/

[47] UCC website: http://www.ucc.ie/en/

[48] LIUC Carlo Cattaneo University website: http://www.liuc.it/default.asp

[49] Blackman Tech College website: http://www.belfastmet.ac.uk/theblackmantech/index.html

[50] The Silver Key Bar and Restaurant website: http://www.thesilverkey.net/

[51] The Gresham Metropole Cork hotel website: http://www.gresham-hotels-cork.com/

[52] Average age of mother, CSO website: http://www.cso.ie/en/statistics/birthsdeathsandmarriages/averageageofmotherclassifiedbymaritalstatus/

[53] Bohan, C.; *For the first time in seven years, Ireland's unemployment rate is under 10%.* thejournal.ie, May 21, 2015; http://www.thejournal.ie/irish-unemployment-rate-2115641-May2015/

[54] Citizens information website: http://www.citizensinformation.ie/en/employment/retirement/older_people_and_working/retirement_age_in_ireland.html

[55] Citizens information website: http://www.citizensinformation.ie/en/justice/criminal_law/criminal_offences/alcohol_and_the_law.html

[56] O'Riordan, S.; *Cork County Council spends €10m on tourism promotion.* Irish Examiner, June 10, 2015; http://www.irishexaminer.com/ireland/cork-county-council-spends-10m-on-tourism-promotion-335566.html

[57] *Tourism Barometer.* Fáilte Ireland, May 2015; http://www.failteireland.ie/FailteIreland/media/WebsiteStructure/Documents/3_Research_Insights/3_General_SurveysReports/REPORT-Failte-Ireland-tourism-barometer-May-2015.pdf?ext=.pdf

[58] The Oliver Plunkett website: http://www.theoliverplunkett.com/

[59] Arthur Mayne website: http://www.corkheritagepubs.com/pubs/arthur-maynes/

[60] Crane Lane Theatre website: http://www.cranelanetheatre.ie/

[61] Orso website: https://www.orso.ie/

[62] L'Atitude 51 website: http://www.latitude51.ie/

[63] The Woodford website: http://www.thewoodford.ie/?q=home

[64] Meades 126 website: http://www.meades126.com/index.html

[65] Il Padrino website: http://www.ilpadrinorestaurant.ie/index.html

[66] Jacques Restaurant website: http://www.jacquesrestaurant.ie/restaurant/home/

[67] Bodega website: http://www.bodegacork.ie/

[68] El Vino website: http://elvino.ie/

[69] An Brog website: http://www.anbrog.com/

[70] Reardens website: http://www.reardens.com/about/

[71] The Long Valley website: http://www.thelongvalleybar.com/

[72] Sin é website: http://www.corkheritagepubs.com/pubs/sin-e/

[73] The Bailey website: http://www.thebaileycork.com/

[74] The Oval website: http://www.corkheritagepubs.com/pubs/the-oval/

[75] Franciscan Well Brewery website: http://www.franciscanwellbrewery.com/

[76] Mutton Lane Inn website: http://www.corkheritagepubs.com/pubs/the-mutton-lane/

[77] Sober Lane website: http://soberlane.com/

[78] Electric website: http://www.electriccork.com/

[79] Cork Bar Furniture website: http://www.corkbarfurniture.ie/

[80] Cork's RedFM website: http://www.redfm.ie/

[81] Cork Independent website: http://www.corkindependent.com/

[82] TripAdvisor website: http://www.tripadvisor.it/

[83] For a detailed list of events in Cork, visit the website: http://cork.ie/events/

[84] Google AdWords website: http://www.google.com/adwords/

[85] MyHome website: https://www.myhome.ie/

[86] Daft website: http://www.daft.ie/

[87] Allsop website: http://www.allsopireland.ie/

[88] Estimate calculated by the following website: http://www.architetto.name/capitolati-preventivi-contratti/calcolo_prezzo_lavori.php

[89] Cork Bar & Catering Equipment Ltd website: http://corkbarandcatering.com/home/

[90] Musgraves website: http://www.musgravemarketplace.ie/

[91] La Cantina di Giorgio website: http://www.lacantinadigiorgio.it/index.html

[92] Enomatic srl website: http://www.enomatic.it/new/default.asp?catIDPadre=41&catID=100

[93] Showine website: http://www.showine.it/

[94] "La Cantina di Giorgio" price list: http://www.lacantinadigiorgio.it/files/LISTINO-PREZZI-VINI---bb---20.pdf

[95] FedEx website: https://www.fedex.com/ratefinder/standalone?method=getQuickQuote

[96] Global Service website: http://www.globalservicespedizioni.it/spedisci-online?source_id=118

[97] TNT website: http://www.tnt.com/express/it_it/site/home.html

[98] Excise duties tables on alcoholic beverages: http://ec.europa.eu/taxation_customs/resources/documents/taxation/excise_duties/alcoholic_beverages/rates/excise_duties-part_i_alcohol_en.pdf

[99] The Boot's Specialities website: http://www.theboot.ie/index.php/home

[100] Bonkers website: http://www.bonkers.ie/compare-gas-electricity-prices/

[101] Irish Water website: http://www.water.ie/

[102] Source: *Low Pay Commission recommends increase in National Minimum Wage of 50 cent to €9.15.* Department of Jobs, Enterprise and Innovation, 21st July 2015; https://www.djei.ie/en/News-And-Events/Department-News/2015/July/21072015.html

[103] Sample calculation mortgage via the website: http://www.mutuionline.it/

[104] Intreo Centre Cork Hanover Street website: http://www.welfare.ie/en/Pages/office/Intreo-Centre-Cork-Hanover-Street.aspx

[105] PPS Number – How to apply website: http://www.welfare.ie/en/Pages/Personal-Public-Service-Number-How-to-Apply.aspx

[106] CRO website: https://www.cro.ie/

[107] Companies Act 2014: http://www.irishstatutebook.ie/eli/2014/act/38/enacted/en/pdf

[108] Private company. Limited by shares only. Part 2 Companies Act 2014

[109] Private company. Can be limited by shares or by guarantee. Part 16 Companies Act 2014

[110] Part 17 Companies Act 2014

[111] Public company. Part 18 Companies Act 2014

[112] Part 19 Companies Act 2014

[113] Schedule 1. Section 19 Companies Act 2014: http://www.irishstatutebook.ie/eli/2014/act/38/schedule/1/enacted/en/html#sched1

[114] Company Search Facility: https://search.cro.ie/company/

[115] Sections 28 and 29 Companies Act 2014

[116] CORE website: https://core.cro.ie/home/index?aspxerrorpath=/Main/index.jsp

[117] Section 151 Companies Act 2014

[118] NACE Code: https://www.cro.ie/Portals/0/Notices/Nace%20code%202.pdf

[119] Section 131 Companies Act 2014

[120] ROS website: https://www.ros.ie/rcw/login/noCertsFound?lang=en